THE CHILDRE... ...R'S ENCYCLOPEDIA OF BIBLE-TEACHING IDEAS:

Old Testament

Group

Loveland, Colorado

The Children's Worker's Encyclopedia of Bible-Teaching Ideas: Old Testament
Copyright © 1997 Group Publishing, Inc.

Credits
Book Acquisitions Editor: Mike Nappa
Editors: Liz Shockey and Susan L. Lingo
Senior Editor: Lois Keffer
Chief Creative Officer: Joani Schultz
Copy Editor: Janis Sampson
Art Director: Lisa Chandler
Assistant Art Director: Kari K. Monson
Cover Art Director: Helen H. Lannis
Cover Designer: Jean Bruns
Illustrators: Amy Bryant and Dana Regan
Production Manager: Ann Marie Gordon

The children's worker's encyclopedia of Bible-teaching ideas. Old
    Testament.
        p.   cm.
    Includes indexes.
    ISBN 1-55945-622-1
    1. Bible. O.T.–Study and teaching–Handbooks, manuals, etc.
2. Christian education of children–Handbooks, manuals, etc.
BS1193.C48 1997
268'.432–dc21

96-46364
                                                            CIP

10 9 8 7 6 5 4 3 2 1   06 05 04 03 02 01 00 99 98 97

Printed in the United States of America.

CONTENTS

CONTRIBUTORS

Many thanks to the following people, who loaned us their creative expertise to help bring together this volume of ideas:

Jody Brolsma
Robin Christy
Leanne Ciampa
Lois Keffer
Susan L. Lingo
Kim Ramos
Linda Shepherd
Liz Shockey
Beth Rowland Wolf

INTRODUCTION

Once upon a time, the editors at a publishing house in Colorado had a dream. "What if," they said, "instead of simply *teaching* kids about the Old Testament, we had a way to help them *experience* and apply the truths found in Scripture?"

So they went right to work. They contacted some of the most creative people in children's ministry and challenged them to develop exciting, inviting Old Testament-based activities and learning experiences for children. Then they compiled those ideas into this volume: *The Children's Worker's Encyclopedia of Bible-Teaching Ideas: Old Testament.*

Suddenly, the book isn't just a dream. It's reality! And it's ready to be shared with children's workers around the world—children's workers like you.

In the following pages, you'll find hundreds of active, guided experiences that take scriptural truths from the Old Testament and bring them to life in your kids. Your children will gain a deeper understanding of the Bible through a variety of sensory and experiential activities including:

 learning games,

 object lessons,

 skits,

 prayers and quiet reflections,

 service projects and missions,

 affirmation activities,

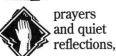 devotions,

 music ideas,

 parties,

 creative storytelling,

 trips 'n' travels,

 and crafts and makables.

With such a wide variety of carefully planned, spiritually focused activities, your children will look forward to spending time with the Bible. Not only will exciting activities spark their interests, but the truths they learn will change their lives.

The Children's Worker's Encyclopedia of Bible-Teaching Ideas: Old Testament is an essential tool for any children's worker interested in helping kids explore and understand the Bible. You can use the book with your group for Sunday school, children's church, midweek meetings, or any other time children are gathered together. So get ready for unique, motivating activities that will inspire your children to learn about the Bible and love the Bible in no time!

GENESIS

*"In the beginning God created
the sky and the earth."*

Genesis 1:1

GENESIS
1:1–2:3

THEME:
God is our creator.

SUMMARY:
This cooperative CRAFT idea uses recyclables to help kids "sculpt" an understanding of God as the only true creator.

PREPARATION: You'll need duct tape, scissors, and a variety of clean recyclable items, such as boxes, plastic lids, aluminum foil scraps, plastic bottles, newspaper, plastic foam cups and plates, and soft drink cans. Before this activity, make sure all recyclables are clean and have no sharp edges.

Set out the recyclables, duct tape, and scissors. Form groups of three to five kids. Say: **It's always interesting to see what can be made from items that most people toss out. You'll have ten minutes to work with your group to "sculpt a masterpiece" from the items you see here. Use duct tape to hold your masterpieces together. When time's up, you'll have a chance to show the entire class what you've made. Have fun!**

As kids make their sculptures, circulate and make comments such as "I'm glad God gave us imaginations to help us make things" and "Imagine what it was like for God to create an entire world!" When kids are finished, gather them together, and have them show their sculptures and tell about them. Affirm each display by leading the class in clapping its approval. Then ask:

- **What could you name your sculptures?**
- **Who decided what to make from the items?**
- **How is this activity like God creating the world?**

Say: **You worked so well in your groups to make these sculptures. But think for a moment: God created the entire world—everything on the earth and above the earth—all by himself! God is our creator, and he did a wondrous job creating everything in the world! You** *made* **sculptures, but God** *created* **the world. Let's read about God's creation.** Read aloud Genesis 1:1–2:3. Then ask:

- **How do you think God felt when he finished his creation?**
- **How was God's act of Creation different from the way you created your sculptures?**

Say: **We're able to use our imaginations and our brains and hands to make things. We take the things God creates and make new things from them. But only God creates. Only God can start with nothing and create an entire world complete with plants, animals, and people! God is the creator and his creation is awesome, isn't it?**

Set the sculptures in the church entrance or a hallway for everyone to look at and enjoy.

GENESIS 2:8–3:24

THEME:
God forgives us because he loves us.

SUMMARY:
Have fun with this interactive, CREATIVE STORYTELLING activity as young children learn about humanity's first sin and God's loving forgiveness.

Say: **We're going to have fun with a unique version of the creation story. Watch carefully, and do what I do.** Read the following story and encourage kids to follow your actions.

IN THE GARDEN

In the beginning God created the world. *(Make a big circle with your arms.)* **And God created a beautiful garden called Eden.** *(Spread arms wide.)* **Let's pretend we're surrounded by the beautiful Garden of Eden. Look at all the lush green plants!** *(Shade your eyes, and look around.)* **Can you smell the flowers?** *(Bend over and sniff.)* **Mmm, they smell so good! And look at all the animals! Look over there!** *(Point.)* **It's a funny monkey. Can you hop up and down like monkeys?** *(Pause.)* **Now turn into friendly lions padding through the garden.** *(Crawl on all fours.)* **And let's not forget the hoppity rabbits!** *(Hop like a rabbit.)*

There were beautiful flowers

and friendly animals in God's special garden. But do you know who else lived there? God made a man named Adam and a woman named Eve to live in the Garden of Eden. Adam, take a bow! *(Have boys bow.)* And Eve, can you wave? *(Have girls wave.)* Adam and Eve lived in the garden and were great friends with God. They loved God, and God loved Adam and Eve very much. *(Give yourself a hug.)*

There were also two very important trees in the Garden of Eden. There was the tree that gives life *(stand tall, hold arms out straight, then point to your heart)*, and the tree that gives the knowledge of good and evil. *(Stand tall, hold arms out straight, then point to your head.)* God told Adam *(shake your finger)*, "You must not eat the fruit from the tree that gives the knowledge of good and evil."

Now in the garden there also lived an evil snake. *(Hiss like a snake.)* The sly serpent told Eve that it wouldn't hurt to eat the fruit of God's tree. *(Hiss like a snake.)* And guess what Adam and Eve did? Adam and Eve disobeyed God and ate that fruit! *(Put your hands to your cheeks, and shake your head.)* All at once, Adam and Eve felt bad—they knew they had done something wrong. They tried to cover themselves and hide from God. *(Crouch down, and cover your eyes.)*

But God loved Adam and Eve, and he looked for them. *(Shade your eyes, and look around.)* God asked if Adam and Eve had eaten the fruit. Adam told God that Eve gave him some of the fruit. Eve said, "Yes, but the snaked tricked me!" God was angry with the serpent. *(Hiss like a snake.)* God told the serpent, "You will crawl on your stomach, and you will eat dust all the days of your life." Can you lie on your tummies and wiggle like a snake? *(Pause.)*

But God still loved Adam and Eve. *(Hug yourself.)* And God forgave them for their sinful disobedience and let them live. God punished Adam and Eve by sending them away from the beautiful garden *(point as if sending someone away)*, but God made clothes for them *(make sewing motions)* and watched over them as they worked in the fields to grow food *(pretend to hoe)*. God loved and forgave Adam and Eve just as God loves and forgives us. *(Hug yourself and smile.)*

GENESIS
3:1-6

THEME:
Don't be fooled by lies.

SUMMARY:
Use this audience-participation SKIT to help children think about choices and their consequences. The skit works best with older children playing the Hostess, Eve, and Monty Serpent; and younger children participating as the Audience.

WHAT'S BEHIND LIE NUMBER ONE?

SCENE: The set of the game show *The Choice Is Yours.*

PROPS: You'll need an empty pie tin, a plate, a knife and fork, and a large cardboard cross. You'll also need a sign that reads "Applause." For the discussion following the skit, you'll need a Bible.

CHARACTERS:
Hostess
Monty Serpent
Eve
Studio Audience

SCRIPT

Hostess: *(Holds up Applause sign. Audience cheers and claps.)*
Monty: Welcome to *The Choice Is Yours!* I'm Monty Serpent, and I will charm you into the deal of your life. Who will our first contestant be?
Eve: *(Jumping up and down and raising her hand.)* Pick me!
Monty: Eve, come on down! Eve, *The Choice Is Yours* is a daring game with a chance for a fabulous prize.
Eve: A fabulous prize? What can I win?
Monty: The stakes are high, Eve. The top prize offers truth, life, and a chance to walk and talk with God!
Hostess: *(Holds up Applause sign. Audience cheers and claps.)*
Eve: And the other?
Monty: That's our zonk prize. It offers death and separation from God.
Eve: *(Shivers.)* I hope I don't bite into that one.

Monty: *(Twirls pretend mustache and gives a villainous laugh.)* We'll see, won't we. Now, Eve, stand here while I show you the possibilities. First, a delicious apple pie. One bite will take you beyond your wildest dreams *(to Audience)* or nightmares.
Hostess: *(Holds up Applause sign. Audience cheers and claps.)*
Eve: Did you say apple? Did it come from that special tree? God told me not to eat fruit from that tree. He said if I ate it or touched it, I would surely die.
Monty: You surely won't die. *(To Audience)* Well, at least not right away. *(To Eve)* Besides, one taste will be a real eye-opener. You will be like God and know good and evil.
Eve: One bite of the pie, and I will be *like* God? Wow! But didn't you say I had another choice? Tell me about that!
Monty: That? That's nothing compared with the taste of my apple pie. *(Pretends to cut a slice and to place it on the plate; hands the plate and the fork to Eve.)* Here, see for yourself. THE CHOICE IS YOURS!
Eve: *(Licking her lips)* Apple pie sounds good to me.
Hostess: *(Holds up Applause sign. Audience cheers and claps.)*
Eve: *(Takes a bite. Drops the plate, choking.)* Monty, you lied to me! Those apples are poisonous!
Monty: Too bad, Eve. *(Laughing wickedly)* When you disobeyed God, you got ZONKED!
Eve: But I wanted truth. I wanted to walk and talk with God.
Monty: You made your choice, Eve. Now you have to live...

er...die with it.

Eve: But is there any way out of this mess?

Monty: Sorry, Eve. There's no way out. Unless, of course *(chuckling wickedly)*, you had a redeemer.

Eve: A redeemer?

Monty: You know, God himself would have to come down here and die in your place. Fat chance of that ever happening. *(Gives a nasty laugh and turns his back.)*

Eve: I wonder... *(Brightens, picks up large cardboard cross. Kneels, and then bows head in sober prayer.)*

Hostess: Life is made up of choices. Choosing to obey God brings life. Choosing to disobey brings death. And the choice is yours!

If you use this skit as a discussion starter, read aloud Genesis 3:1-6, then ask:

● **What did Eve lose when she chose to disobey God?**

● **What were the lies the serpent used to trick Eve?**

● **Can we still be fooled by the enemy's lies? How?**

● **What kinds of consequences will we face if we disobey God today?**

● **Why did Christ, God's Son, have to die on the cross for us?**

GENESIS 6:5-22

THEME:
It's important to obey God.

SUMMARY:
This hands-on OBJECT LESSON helps older kids "build" their concept of obeying God no matter how big the task.

PREPARATION: You'll need different-colored markers and scraps of wood from a lumber store or construction site. Wooden slats, blocks, circles, dowel-rod portions, and other odd shapes and pieces work well. You'll also need a Bible.

Place the wood pieces and markers on the floor, and have kids sit in a circle around them.

Say: **Let's have a little creative fun and see how well you follow directions.** Give kids the following directions, pausing for them to complete each task.

● **Choose a piece of wood and a marker.**

● **Write the word "God" on one side of your wood.**

● **Place the wood on your head and shake hands with the people on both sides of you.**

● **Make three different-colored squiggles on one side of your wood.**

● **Stand up, balance your piece of wood on your nose, and whistle the tune to "Happy Birthday to You."**

● **Sit down, and write the word "obey" on your wood.**

● Get on your hands and knees, put your wood on your back, crawl all the way around the circle, then sit down in your own place again.

● Draw a happy face somewhere on your piece of wood.

Say: **Good job!** Then ask:

● Did you follow every direction? Why or why not?

● How did you feel when the direction seemed a little silly?

Say: **Sometimes it's hard to follow directions when we don't understand why we're doing them. Let's read about a man who followed God's directions even when he didn't understand.** Read the story of Noah building the ark from Genesis 6:5-22. Then ask:

● How do you think Noah felt when God told him to build a big boat on dry land?

● Why did Noah obey?

Say: **Noah obeyed God—even when God's directions seemed puzzling. And because Noah obeyed God, God saved Noah's life and the lives of his family and the animals. God wants us to obey him, and he honors our obedience. The words on your piece of wood say, "Obey God." Take your wood piece home as a reminder that we can trust and obey God even when we don't understand his directions.**

GENESIS
6:5–7:1

THEME:
Following God is more important than being popular.

SUMMARY:
This audience-participation SKIT helps children recognize the importance of listening and following God. It works best with older children as the actors. Encourage younger children to participate as the Audience.

TAKE ME OUT TO THE ARK

SCENE: A broadcast booth and a cutaway interview with Noah.

PROPS: You'll need to make signs that say: "Cheer," "Laugh," "Rain," "Help," and "Boo." You'll also need Bibles for the discussion following the skit.

CHARACTERS:
Announcer
Audience
Coach Rotten
Coach Rudely
Reporter Sid Spoiler
Noah

SCRIPT

Announcer: It's a beautiful day for a ballgame—not a cloud in the sky. As usual, Scoffer Stadium is filled with fans fighting for the best seats. Let's hear it for the guy who just shoved a sweet little old lady out of her seat by third base. *(Holds up Cheer sign.)*
Audience: Yea!
Announcer: Today's game is

between the Scoffers and the Wickeds. The start of the game has been delayed because someone has *stolen* all the bases! Isn't that great? *(Holds up Cheer sign.)*

Audience: Yea!

Announcer: I have the coaches of both teams here in the booth. Coach Rotten, what's your strategy for beating the Wickeds?

Rotten: Our pitchers have found a new way to doctor up the ball. The Wickeds won't get a single hit off us. Cheat 'em and beat 'em—that's our motto!

Announcer: How about you, Coach Rudely?

Rudely: Ha! We've done better than that. We paid off the home plate umpire! This game is in the bag.

Announcer: Well, as we say in the business, "Never dare to play fair!" Just before the opening pitch, we have late-breaking news from Noah's ark. I'm sure you've all heard of the famous boat that's too big to float. Let's go live to our reporter Sid Spoiler, who's at the scene. *(Reporter and Noah enter.)*

Reporter: Hey, Noah, isn't it bad enough you built a ship that can't sail? Now I see you're loading it with animals. Pew-wee! Why make a stink in the middle of our fair city?

Noah: Our city isn't so fair. No one cares about doing what's right.

Reporter: That's right, Noah. We're all just here for a good time. Are you aware that everyone thinks you're a first-class wacko?

Noah: It's not important to me what people think, Sid. God told me . . .

Announcer: *(Holds up Laugh sign.)*

Audience: *(Laughs.)*

Reporter: You heard it here, folks. Our gray-haired neighbor's strange behavior continues. He thinks God has been talking to him! Tell me, Noah, what does God look like?

Announcer: *(Holds up Laugh sign.)*

Audience: *(Laughs.)*

Noah: As I was saying, the Lord told me he was going to destroy the earth with a flood, and . . .

Announcer: *(Holds up Laugh sign.)*

Audience: *(Laughs.)*

Reporter: You've been saying that for months, old man. It ain't gonna happen.

Noah: Believe what you will—I'll do what God tells me.

Reporter: As they say, folks, truth *is* stranger than fiction. Now back to Scoffer Stadium where the big game is about to begin. *(Reporter and Noah exit.)*

Announcer: Thanks for the report, Sid. I'd like to hear what our two baseball coaches think of Noah.

Rotten: Can you believe the nerve of that guy? Telling us that our game is gonna be rained out!

Rudely: That's one thing we can finally agree on, Rotten. The guy's crazy.

Rotten: Yeah, maybe we should send him on a cruise to the end of the world!

Announcer: *(Interrupting)* News bulletin! Dark clouds are forming on the horizon just north of

Scoffer Stadium. Hang on, folks, we have another update from Sid Spoiler at the ark. *(Reporter enters.)*

Reporter: Sid Spoiler, here. Noah and his family have just entered the ark, and the door is closing all by itself! It's the strangest thing I've ever seen. It's getting awfully dark, and rain is beginning to fall steadily. *(Runs for cover on stage.)*

Announcer: That's not what we wanted to hear! It looks like that storm system is beginning to move in on the stadium. *(Holds up Rain sign.)*

Audience: *(Begins to slap their thighs to make the sound of rain. Continue through end of skit.)*

Announcer: Sorry, baseball fans, but it looks like the big game just got rained out. *(Holds up Boo sign.)*

Audience: Boo!

Announcer: Back to Sid. Sid? Come in, Sid!

Reporter: The rain is coming down in buckets! The water is waist-deep and rising. *(Pounding on imaginary door)* Hey, Noah! Open up! Please, let me in. Help! *(Exits.)*

Announcer: *(Holds up Help sign.)*

Audience: Help!

Announcer: Sid, are you still there? Sid? Wow, this is looking bad. Look at that rain come down. Sports fans, I'm signing off. *Run for high ground!*

If you use this skit as a discussion starter, first read aloud Genesis 6:5–7:1, then ask:

● **How do you think Noah's neighbors felt about him?**

● **Why did Noah choose to obey God?**

● **When have people laughed at you for doing what's right?**

● **Why do people ignore what God wants them to do?**

● **How can we help people believe in God?**

GENESIS 8:18–9:1, 8-17

THEME:
God keeps his promises.

SUMMARY:
This active DEVOTION teaches kids that God never breaks his promises.

PREPARATION: You'll need tape and a twig or small tree branch for each child. You'll also need a Bible.

EXPERIENCE

Place the twigs at one end of the room. Gather kids in a circle at the opposite end of the room. Say: **Think for a moment about promises you've made to others or that others have made to you.** Ask:

● **Who can tell about a promise you made?**

● **Did you keep your promise? Why or why not?**

● **How does it feel if you**

break a promise?

Say: **The twigs at the other end of the room are pretend promises. When I say "go," hop to the twigs, break one, then bring both pieces of the broken twig back to the circle.**

When all the kids are back in the circle, pass around the tape, and challenge each child to tape his or her twig back together.

RESPONSE

When all the twigs are "repaired," ask:

● **How easy was it to break your twig?**

● **Was it easy or hard to repair? Explain.**

● **Is the repaired twig as strong as it was before it was broken? Why or why not?**

Say: **These twigs are like promises. If they're broken, the strength is gone—they can never be made as good as new. God knows how important promises are. Let's read about a special promise God made to Noah. Listen carefully, and see if you think God has ever broken this promise.** Let volunteers take turns reading aloud Genesis 8:18–9:1, 8-17. Then ask:

● **What promise did God make to Noah?**

● **Do you think that promise is for us as well? Why or why not?**

● **Who can tell us about some of God's promises from the Bible?**

CLOSING

Say: **God always keeps his promises. And God wants us to honor our promises just as he** honors his. **Let's pray and ask God's help in keeping promises.** Pray: **Dear God, please help us keep our word just as you keep yours. In Jesus' name, amen.**

Take your twigs home to remind you that broken promises hurt and to remind you that God always keeps his promises.

GENESIS
11:1-9

THEME:
God is in charge of his world.

SUMMARY:
In this exciting LEARNING GAME, kids see that people who think they're as smart as God are just fooling themselves.

PREPARATION: You'll need one pack of index cards for every eight to ten children. You'll also need Bibles.

Set the index cards on the floor. Gather the kids around the cards, and say: **We're going to play a building game. You'll work as an entire group to build one tall tower from these cards. You'll have three minutes to build your tower, but you can't use regular words to talk to each other. You may only say "ooga-hooga" to communicate with one another. You may begin building now.**

Give kids three minutes to build their tower. Then call time and ask:

● **What was it like trying to**

build a tower without being able to talk to one another in words you understood?

● How would talking in a language that you knew have helped?

Say: **People in Old Testament times thought they could build a tower all the way to heaven. But God had other plans. Let's read the story from the Bible to find out why God didn't like this tower and what he did about it. When you know what God did to stop the tower from being built, clap your hands one time.**

Ask volunteers to read aloud Genesis 11:1-9. Then ask:

● **Why did the people in the story want to build a great tower?**

● **Why did God stop the tower from being built?**

● **What did God do to make sure something like this would never happen again?**

Say: **The people in this story thought they were pretty smart. They wanted to build a tower that reached all the way to heaven to show how powerful they were. But God wanted the people to know that** *he* **was in charge! So God mixed up their languages so that they couldn't team up to build another tower that high. Then God scattered the people all around the earth. God taught the people that he was in charge of everything—and we know that God is in charge of all we do.**

Now let's knock over the tower we've made and shout, "God's in charge!"

GENESIS 12:1-5

THEME:
God has a plan for our lives.

SUMMARY:
This unusual CRAFT idea reminds kids that God has mapped out a perfect plan for each of our lives.

PREPARATION: You'll need small blocks of wood, old road maps or atlas pages, scissors, white craft glue, water, a plastic bowl, a plastic tablecloth, sandpaper, and paintbrushes. You'll also need a Bible.

Before class, collect scraps of wood from a lumber store or construction site. The wood scraps don't need to be the same size, but make sure each one has a side that is at least three-by-three inches. If you have younger kids, pre-cut old map or atlas pages into three-inch squares to fit on the wood scraps. Older kids will enjoy cutting out their own "maps" to fit their wood pieces. You'll also need to mix two parts white craft glue to one part water in a plastic bowl.

Cover a table with a plastic tablecloth. Then set out sandpaper, maps and map pieces, scissors, markers, the glue mixture, and paintbrushes. Have each child choose a piece of wood and a map. Have kids sand away rough edges, then choose which side of the wood they'd like to glue their map pieces to. Demonstrate how to brush a light coat of the glue mixture onto the wood, press a map piece in place, then brush a light coat of the glue mixture over the map piece.

As kids work, say: **We usually have good maps to help us find where we're going.** Ask:

● **When have you used a map to help you get somewhere?**

● **Can you tell us about a time when you got lost because you didn't have a map?**

When kids have finished, have them set their map blocks in a sunny place to dry. Then gather kids in a circle, and have a volunteer read aloud Genesis 12:1-5. Ask:

● **Who showed Abraham and his family where to go?**

● **Do you think God gave Abraham a map?**

● **Why do you think Abraham obeyed God?**

● **How do you think Abraham and his family felt about going to a strange new land?**

Say: **God had a plan for Abraham's life. Abraham obeyed God, and God made him the father of many nations. God has plans for our lives, too. And when we follow God's plan, God can do wonderful things through us!** Ask:

● **Who can tell about some special ways God might use us?**

Say: **Use your map block as a reminder that God has a wonderful plan for you and that the very best thing you can do is follow God!**

TEACHER TIPS
Using a hand-held hair dryer will speed up drying time for the wood blocks. You may wish to have kids glue tiny plastic cars to the tops of the blocks for a fun touch.

GENESIS
17:1-5

THEME:
God knows all about us.

SUMMARY:
Play this fun LEARNING GAME to teach kids that God knows everything about us.

PREPARATION: You'll need paper towels, paper cups, and alphabet cereal. You'll also need a watch, a Bible, and a book that tells the meaning of names. Before this game, fill the paper cups with the alphabet cereal. Prepare a paper cup for each child in class.

Have kids form groups of three. Hand each child a paper towel and cup containing alphabet letters. Say: **Think of some names of people you know. You'll have five minutes to work together in your trios to form as many names and nicknames as you can using the alphabet letters in your cups. Use your paper towel to put the letters on. Ready? Go!**

Call time at the end of five minutes. Let each group read the names they've spelled. Then say: **Let's have fun finding out what your names mean.** Look up the meaning of several children's names. Then have a volunteer read aloud Genesis 17:1-5. Ask:

● **What new name did God give Abram?**

● **Why did God give Abram a new name?**

Say: **Sometimes we like to be**

called fun nicknames. Some people like to shorten their names. Robert might like to be called Bob, or we might call someone Liz instead of Elizabeth. But God didn't change Abram's name just for fun. God changed Abram's name to Abraham because God knew that Abraham would have a son, and Abraham's son would have children, and Abraham's grandsons would have children, and those children would have children, and before long, Abraham's family would spread all over the world! God knew all about Abraham, and God knows all about us, too. Ask:

● **How does it feel to know that God knows all about you?**

● **What are some things that God knows about you that you don't even know?**

Say: **Spell out the name of the one who knows all about us, then gobble up all your letters!**

GENESIS 18:1-16; 21:1-3

THEME:
Nothing is impossible for God.

SUMMARY:
This "impossible" DEVOTION is exciting for kids and helps them to remember that *nothing* is impossible for our all-powerful God!

PREPARATION: You'll need balloons, clear tape, permanent mark-ers, and a straight pin. You'll also need a Bible.

EXPERIENCE
This is a great devotion for older kids. You may wish to choose another activity if you have very young children who might be upset if a balloon pops.

Blow up and tie off a balloon for each child in class. Set out permanent markers and transparent tape. Hand children each a balloon, and invite them to use the markers to draw smiley faces on their balloons. Then give each child a two-inch piece of tape to stick on the balloon.

Hold up the straight pin. Say: **It seems impossible to poke a balloon with a pin and not have it pop, doesn't it? But when we trust in God, we know that nothing is impossible.** Demonstrate how to carefully push a straight pin into the center of the tape on a balloon. Be sure the pin goes straight into the tape. The tape should resist the pin and keep the balloon from popping. Carefully remove the pin, and place another piece of tape over the pinhole.

Let kids take turns pushing the pin into the tape on the balloons, then covering the pinholes with more tape.

RESPONSE
When everyone has had a turn, set the pin aside and ask:

● **Did you think this trick was too hard to do? Why or why not?**

● **Is anything too big or hard for God? Explain.**

● **What happens when we trust God with our problems?**

Read aloud Genesis 18:1-16.

Then ask:
- **What did God promise Abraham and Sarah?**
- **Why did Sarah think having a baby was impossible?**

Say: **Let's see what happened.** Read aloud Genesis 21:1-3.

CLOSING

Say: **Nothing is impossible for God because God is all-powerful. Even if something looks impossible to us, God can make things turn out great!**
- **What's one problem you can trust God to help you with this week?**

Say: **Let's join hands and say a prayer. We'll ask God to help us remember that all things are possible through him.** Pray: **Dear God, we thank you for being strong and wise and more powerful than anyone or anything. Please help us to trust you with all our problems and to remember that nothing is impossible with you! In Jesus' name, amen.**

GENESIS
21:1-8

THEME:
We can trust God's Word.

SUMMARY:
With this MUSIC IDEA, kids will bop 'n' hop to a rhythm 'n' rhyme—and learn how to spell "promise" at the same time.

PREPARATION: You'll need seven index cards and a marker. You'll also need a Bible. Before this activity, write each letter of the word "PROMISE" on a separate index card.

Gather kids in a group, and hand seven kids each a letter card. Have the Card Kids stand in front of the group.

Say: **Let's have a fun time with rhythm 'n' rhyme! We'll rap out the words to a rhyme about God's promises. As we spell the word "promise," the Card Kids will hold out their letters. The rest of us will say the words to a rappin' rhyme.**

Teach kids the following rhyme. Then have kids do a clap-stomp rhythm as they call out the letters for the word "promise."

> **P-R-O-M-I-S-E!**
> **God gives promises to you and me.**
> **God keeps them all—just wait and see.**
> **P-R-O-M-I-S-E!**

Say: **Now let's start dropping letters. When we repeat the rhyme, clap instead of saying the letter P. The next time through we'll clap on P and R. We'll keep going until we've clapped out the word "promise" without saying a letter!**

When you've finished, have a volunteer read aloud Genesis 21:1-8. Ask:
- **Why did Sarah doubt God's promise at first?**
- **Do you think Sarah ever doubted God again? Why or why not?**

Say: **When God makes a**

promise, he always keeps it. God never breaks a promise because he loves us. That's why we can trust God's Word! Teach the promise rap to your family this evening, and talk about how God keeps his promises.

GENESIS 24:10-27

THEME:
God tests our faithfulness.

SUMMARY:
Participating in this CRAFT gives kids the opportunity to make bouquets of love.

PREPARATION: You'll need individually wrapped candies, scissors, white thread, and ribbon. You'll also need artificial flowers for all the residents in a care center or nursing home.

Set out candies, scissors, thread, and the artificial flowers. Demonstrate how to tie the thread to one end of a candy wrapper, then tie the candy in the center of an artificial flower. If you have young children, you may wish to use thin ribbon instead of thread. Explain to kids that they're making colorful treats to brighten the day of those who need a cheerful gift.

Help children attach the candies to the flowers. Point out that the sweet treats in the center of the flowers are like the loving hearts in God's people. Make comments such

as "God wants us to love others" and "When we offer love to other people, we're offering love to God."

When the candy flowers are finished, have kids help gather them into large bouquets and tie the bouquets with ribbon. Then gather the children, and ask a volunteer to read aloud Genesis 24:10-27. Ask:
● **What job did Abraham give his servant?**
● **How did the servant ask God to help him?**
● **How did Rebekah show kindness to Abraham's servant?**
● **Why did she do it?**
Say: Rebekah knew that Abraham's servant and his camels were tired and thirsty, so she did something kind for them. She wasn't looking for anything in return, but God rewarded her kindness. Today we've made special treats for people we don't know. Ask:
● **How do you think God feels when people do kind things for each other?**
● **Will we get any special reward for doing this?**
Say: When we do kind things for people, we don't expect a reward. The best reward is knowing that we've shared God's love with people and brightened their day. I'll be sure these treats get to people who can use lots of love! Choose a candy that you can enjoy on your way home.

Be sure to deliver the treats to a care facility. If you have time, invite the kids to go along and sing songs to the residents to share even more of their love!

GENESIS
25:29-34

THEME:
God's gifts are treasures.

SUMMARY:
In this SKIT, a thirsty child almost trades his new bike for a sip of ice-cold lemonade.

ESAU SLURPED THE SOUP!

SCENE: A boy makes an important choice at a lemonade stand.

PROPS: You'll need a table, a tablecloth, a napkin, two chairs, a pitcher, paper cups, and a bike.

CHARACTERS:
Jessica
Blake
Jared

SCRIPT

Jessica: *(Sitting with Blake at lemonade stand)* Get your lemonade here!

Blake: Just twenty-five cents to cool off!

Jared: *(Comes up to the stand pushing his bike.)* It sure is hot! *(Licks lips.)* I'd give anything for a glass of lemonade.

Blake: All we're asking is a quarter.

Jared: A quarter? No can do, Blake. I'm broke.

Jessica: Too bad, Jared. *(Looks around.)* Next?

Jared: You don't understand, Jess. I just rode ten blocks in one-hundred-degree heat. I'm dying here. I'll pay you a quarter tomorrow, OK?

Jessica: You already owe me seventy-five cents!

Jared: How about you, Blake? How about giving me a break?

Blake: Sorry, Jared, if you want a glass of our ice-cold lemonade, you're going to have to cut us a deal.

Jared: What kind of deal?

Blake: How about trading us something for our lemonade?

Jared: Man, I'm so thirsty, I'd give you everything I own for a sip!

Blake: Everything? How about just your bike?

Jared: *(Looks at bike, stunned.)* My wheels?

Blake: You said you were willing to give us everything. And we've got fresh-squeezed lemonade. Do you want some or not?

Jared: *(Eyes the lemonade greedily.)* It does sound tempting...

Jessica: Jared, you wouldn't trade us your treasure, your new mountain bike, for a glass of lemonade, would you?

Jared: I don't know, Jess. I'm so thirsty I might die!

Jessica: Why, Jared, you remind me of Esau!

Jared: Who's that?

Jessica: Let me show you. *(She takes the tablecloth and drapes it over her head.)* It's like this. The Bible tells a story about twin brothers named Esau and Jacob. One day Jacob was cooking a pot of vegetable soup.

Jared: It's too hot for soup!

Jessica: Anyway *(kneels down and pretends to be stirring a big pot over a camp fire)*, Esau had been hunting all day and hadn't had a bite to eat. When he smelled that soup, it made his stomach growl!

Blake: I remember what happens. *(Grabs the napkin and holds it to his chin like a beard, then acts out the part of Esau.)* Give me a bowl of that soup—I'm starving!

Jessica: Sorry, Esau. You'll have to cook your own soup.

Blake: But I'm starving, Jacob! If you give me a bowl, I'll give you everything I own!

Jessica: You'll give me everything, including what Dad is saving for you?

Blake: Quit fooling around, Jacob. I told you I was starving. I'll give you all you ask—just give me that soup!

Jared: *(Interrupting)* That seems like a pretty silly thing for Esau to do.

Jessica: He was pretty silly if you ask me. He gave up everything he owned for something he could have made himself.

Blake: Now about that bike, Jared.

Jared: No deal, Blake. I'm going home to make my own pitcher of lemonade.

If you use this skit as a discussion starter, here are possible questions:

● Why would it have been foolish for Jared to trade his new bike for a glass of lemonade?

● Why is Jared's bike like a treasure to him?

● What treasures has God given us?

● When is it OK to give away something important to us?

GENESIS 27:1-33

THEME:
God wants us to be happy for others, not jealous.

SUMMARY:
Use this interactive, CREATIVE STORYTELLING idea to help kids learn that tricking people is wrong.

THE STOLEN BLESSING

Before telling this story, go over the following cue words and actions with the children. Each time they hear one of the cue words listed below, have them act out the motion that accompanies that word.

● hairy—Shake head.
● smooth—Rub palms together.
● wrinkly—Wrinkle nose and hop one time.
● slippery—Sit down, then pop up.
● boo—Cup hands around mouth and boo.

Say: **Long ago a man named Isaac and his wife Rebekah had twin sons. Their names were Jacob and Esau. By the time the boys had grown up, they looked very different. Esau had hairy arms, but Jacob's arms were smooth.**

When the twins' father was old and wrinkly, he wanted to give his hairy son, Esau, a special blessing. Special blessings were for the oldest boys in the family, and Esau had been born a few moments before Jacob.

Hairy Esau was excited about the blessing. But Jacob was jealous! So he decided to play a very slippery trick on his brother Esau. Jacob planned to steal the blessing meant for his brother! Boo!

Jacob knew his father was old and wrinkly and couldn't see very well. So Jacob glued goat fur to his smooth hands and neck so he'd feel hairy like Esau. Then Jacob went to dish up a steaming bowl of slippery soup to take to his father.

When Isaac's wrinkly hand touched Jacob's hairy hand, Isaac thought it was Esau! So Isaac gave Jacob his special blessing. Jacob had tricked his father and his brother and received the blessing. Boo! Jacob stole his brother's blessing with a very slippery trick!

When Esau found out what Jacob had done, Esau made plans to kill his slippery brother. So Jacob had to run away and live apart from his family for twenty years!

GENESIS
37:2-36

THEME:
God wants us to love our families.

SUMMARY:
Use this creative PRAYER to help kids focus on the love their families share.

PREPARATION: You'll need napkins and red finger gelatin cut into heart shapes. You'll also need a Bible. Before class, prepare heart-shaped finger gelatin using the recipe below.

FINGER GELATIN
Mix 2 packages of strawberry-flavored gelatin with 1½ cups of water. Pour into a 9×13 pan, and chill until firm. Using a heart-shaped cookie cutter, cut a gelatin heart for each child in class.

Gather children in a circle. Read aloud the story of Joseph and his brothers from Genesis 37:2-36. When you're finished reading, ask:

● **Why did Joseph's brothers put him in a well?**

● **If you had been one of Joseph's brothers would you have been jealous of him? Why or why not?**

● **Have you ever been jealous of someone? Explain.**

Say: **Sometimes things don't seem fair in our families and sometimes we may wonder if our brothers and sisters are loved more than we are. But God wants family members to love each other equally. We're all part of God's family, and God loves each one of us.** Ask:

● **How can you show the people in your family that you love them this week?**

Encourage kids to mention thoughtful actions such as helping one another, showing forgiveness, and saying kind words to each other.

Hand each child a gelatin heart on a napkin. Say: **Let's go around** the circle and say the names of the people in our families. As you peek through your gelatin heart, say their names and end by saying, "I love you."

When everyone has had a turn, say: **Let's offer a prayer for our families.** Pray: **Dear God, thank you for giving us families. Help us show each person in our families how much we appreciate and love them. In Jesus' name, amen.** Let kids enjoy eating their treats.

GENESIS
45:1-15

THEME:
We can forgive others.

SUMMARY:
With this MUSIC IDEA, kids sing a snappy song and learn that forgiveness means *giving* love.

PREPARATION: You'll need scissors and colorful crepe paper. You'll also need Bibles. Before this activity, cut two two-foot crepe paper streamers for each child.

Have volunteers read aloud Genesis 45:1-15. Let each volunteer read one verse aloud. Have someone read verse 15 a second time. Then ask:

● **How did Joseph show that he had forgiven his brothers?**

● **Why do you think Joseph forgave them for the awful things they'd done to him?**

● Would you have forgiven them? Explain.

Say: **It's easy to be angry with someone, but it's not always easy to be forgiving. To forgive someone, you need to give a lot of love. But God wants us to forgive others—and he wants us to love others, too. Did you know that in the word "forgive" is the little word "give"? Maybe it's there to remind us we need to give love to be forgiving!**

Hand out the streamers, and say: **Let's sing a song about putting the "G-I-V-E" back into the word "forgive." You can wave your pompom streamers as we sing.**

Lead kids in singing "Put the G-I-V-E Back" to the tune of "Old MacDonald Had a Farm." Encourage kids to joyously wave their streamers as you sing.

> **Put the G-I-V-E back into the word "forgive!"**
> **That's the way our loving God wants M-E, me to live!**
> **I can care.**
> **I can share.**
> **Show my love**
> **Ev'rywhere!**
> **Put the G-I-V-E back into the word "forgive!"**
> (Repeat)

When you're finished singing, say: **That was great! Now let's give three cheers for forgiveness!** Lead kids in three rousing cheers, encouraging them to wave their streamers.

GENESIS
50:15-21

THEME:
God wants us to forgive.

SUMMARY:
In this SKIT, a courtroom drama unfolds: The prosecuting attorney, played by an older child, presents evidence to show why Joseph should not forgive his brothers.

YOUR VERDICT, PLEASE

SCENE: Joseph's brothers are judged harshly.

PROPS: You'll need two chairs, a gavel (a meat mallet or hammer), and a desk or table.

CHARACTERS:
Lawyer
Judge
Eli the Slave Trader
Simeon
Joseph

SCRIPT

Lawyer: *(Speaking dramatically with arms waving)* Your Honor, Joseph's brothers are criminals! Years ago these brothers sold Joseph as a slave! To cover their crime, they told their father that Joseph was dead. These brothers deserve to be punished!

Judge: *(Sitting behind the desk or table facing the audience)* You may call your first witness.

Lawyer: I call Eli the Slave Trader. *(Sitting in a chair facing the audience)* Tell us about the morning in question. You were leading your caravan when you saw shepherds with their sheep. What happened?

Eli: One of those shepherds—Simeon, I think—flagged me down. He said he had a slave he wanted to sell. When they pulled the boy out of the dry well, I realized they were selling their own brother!

Lawyer: *(Spoken dramatically.)* Their brother, you say?

Eli: Yes, sir.

Lawyer: Can you remember Joseph's reaction?

Eli: It was like this...
(Eli freezes, and the scene moves to the selling of Joseph.)

Simeon: *(Holding Joseph by the arm and shaking him.)* Ha, Joseph, we're getting rid of you at last! We've had enough of your wild dreams and stories about how we, your brothers, will someday bow down to you.

Joseph: Can I help my dreams? I love you all, brothers. Please don't hurt me.

Simeon: Hurt you? We were planning to kill you. But now we have a better plan. *(Throws Joseph at the feet of Eli, who has risen from the chair and taken his place in the scene.)* He's all yours, Slave Trader.

Joseph: No, Simeon, don't do this! *(Eli grabs Joseph by the arm and drags him away. Joseph calls over his shoulder.)* I love you all, brothers.
(Joseph returns to the audience, and the scene changes back to the courtroom.)

Lawyer: Your Honor, Joseph has suffered terribly because of the crime his brothers committed against him. He missed his father. He worked long, hard hours as a slave in the house of Potiphar. He was accused of a crime he did not commit and spent many long years in jail. But today, no thanks to his brothers, Joseph has risen above all that. He's second in command to the king of Egypt. Your Honor, lock these brothers in the same jail that held Joseph as prisoner—and throw away the key! What is your verdict?

Judge: I find the defendants *guilty! (Pounds the gavel on the table.)*

Joseph: *(Rising from the audience)* May I address the court, your Honor?

Judge: You may, Joseph.

Joseph: All that has been said today is true. My brothers sold me into slavery when I was a boy. But don't you see? What they planned for evil, God used for good.

Judge: Still, your brothers deserve to be punished.

Joseph: I understand, your Honor. But I have forgiven them, and I demand that they be set free.

Simeon: *(Runs to Joseph and bows to him.)* I do not deserve to be forgiven, my brother.

Joseph: *(Helps Simeon rise to his feet.)* That may be true, but I forgive you anyway.

If you use this skit as a discussion starter, here are possible questions:

● **Did Joseph's brothers deserve forgiveness? Why or why not?**

● **Why does God forgive us for the wrong things we do?**

● **Why is it important for us to forgive others?**

● **How can we forgive those who hurt us?**

Exodus

" 'I am the God of your ancestors—the God of
Abraham, the God of Isaac, and the God of
Jacob.' "

Exodus 3:6a

EXODUS
1:8-22

THEME:
God helps us when we're faithful.

SUMMARY:
This exciting LEARNING GAME, a variation of dodge ball, teaches kids what it means to receive help.

PREPARATION: You'll need masking tape and a playground ball or soft foam ball. You'll also need a Bible. This game is best suited for a gym or open playground. Use masking tape to divide the playing area in half.

Form two teams, and have them stand on opposite sides of the center line. Tell the kids in each team to form pairs.

Say: **The object of this game is to tag the opposing team's players with the ball as you try to keep from being tagged yourself. You'll toss the ball back and forth across the line, always below the waist. You'll need to lock elbows with your partner. If you're tagged on the arm, that arm is frozen for the rest of the game. If you're tagged on the leg, you can't stand on that leg for the rest of the game—you'll have to hop on the other leg. Partners may help each other stand and move. But if both your legs are tagged, you and your partner must sit out for the rest of the game.**

Play until all the players on one team are out. Then have kids take three deep breaths, reach high in the air, touch their toes, and gather in a circle. Ask:

● **How did having a partner make this game easier?**

Say: **You and your partner did a good job of helping each other. Listen for the helpers' names in this Bible story.** Read aloud Exodus 1:8-22. Then ask:

● **Who helped the Israelite babies stay alive?**

● **Why do you think the nurses went against Pharaoh's orders and helped the Israelite babies stay alive?**

● **What did God do for the women who helped the Israelite babies?**

● **Can you tell us about a time when a friend helped you even though you knew it was hard?**

Say: **We all need help from our friends—the friends God provides. And God helps both us and our friends because he loves us so much. We can count on each other for help just as we did in our game. And it can help us remember that we can always count on God!**

Have kids form new teams and play one more round of the game.

EXODUS 2:1-10

THEME:
God protects us because he loves us.

SUMMARY:
With this CREATIVE STORY-TELLING idea, kids help tell the Bible story and learn how God protected Moses at birth.

THE BABY BUNDLE

As you tell this story, have kids listen for the following cue words and do the accompanying motions when they hear the words.

● Israelite—Hold up a fist.

● God—Clap twice and say, "the Lord!"

● Pharaoh—Boo and hiss.

● baby—Rock a pretend baby, and say "wah."

An <u>Israelite</u> woman and her family lived in Egypt. The woman loved <u>God</u> very much, but the wicked ruler of Egypt didn't love <u>God</u> at all. The wicked ruler was called <u>Pharaoh</u>. <u>Pharaoh</u> decided there were too many <u>Israelites</u> in the land. He decided to have all the <u>baby</u> boys killed.

The <u>Israelite</u> woman had a <u>baby</u> boy. She hid the <u>baby</u> for three months. But then she couldn't hide him anymore, so she wove a basket and laid the <u>baby</u> inside. Then she carefully placed the basket at the edge of the Nile River. The <u>baby</u> floated in his basket while his sister watched to see what would happen.

Soon Pharaoh's daughter came down to the river to take a bath. The princess saw the floating basket and told one of her slave girls to bring it to her. What do you think happened then? The princess peeked in the basket and saw the baby! She felt sorry for him. "This baby belongs to the Israelites," she said.

Just then the baby's sister ran up and offered to find someone to take care of him. "Yes, go!" said the princess. So the girl brought the baby's own mother to the princess. "Take care of him until he's older," the princess commanded.

When the baby grew older, the Israelite woman gave him back to the princess and from that day on he grew up in the palace. The princess named him Moses. And when Moses grew up, he helped set the Israelites free from cruel Pharaoh. Yea, God!

EXODUS
2:1-10

THEME:
God takes care of us.

SUMMARY:
In this melodramatic SKIT, baby Moses is discovered by a princess.

BABY IN A BASKET

SCENE: Baby Moses is saved by his mother and sister.

PROPS: You'll need tissues, a basket or box, and a baby doll. You'll also need a Bible for the discussion after the skit.

CHARACTERS:
Pharaoh
Miriam
Princess
Servant
Mom
Audience

SCRIPT

Pharaoh: (Holds the tissue above his lips like a mustache.) Ha, ha, ha! I, the villainous Pharaoh, say *death* to all baby boys!

Audience: Boo!

Miriam: (Holds tissue in her hair like a bow.) Say it isn't so! Oh, help, help, my baby brother!

Audience: (Clasps hands to cheeks.) Oh, no!

Mom: (Holds tissue and weeps.) Boohoo, boohoo! Miriam, quick! We have to hide baby Moses. Let's put him in this basket-boat I made. (Puts doll in basket.) I'll float him on the river! (Sets basket down.)

Miriam: (Shields eyes with hand.) Good, I'll watch him from the bank!

Audience: (Clasps hands to hearts.) Our hero!

Mom: (Blows her nose into tissue.) Don't go to the bank. I forgot my checkbook!

Audience: (Clasps hands to cheeks.) Oh, no!

Miriam: (Continues to hold bow in her hair throughout skit.) I don't mean the First Bank of Egypt. I mean the bank of the Nile River!

Mom: (Gasps.) Quiet, someone is coming!

Audience: *(Clasps hands to cheeks.)* Oh, no!

Princess: *(Pretending to take a swim nearby, waves the tissue theatrically.)* Look at that. Honey, fetch that cute little ol' basket for me.

Miriam: *(From her hiding place)* Uh-oh, this could be curtains!

Audience: *(Clasp hands to cheeks.)* Oh, no!

Servant: *(Swims to basket and wipes it off with tissue.)* Here you go, miss.

Princess: *(Continues to wave tissue throughout skit. She looks inside the basket.)* Oh look, a cute little baby. *(Picks doll up by its foot.)* I think I'll keep him.

Audience: *(Clapping)* Yea!

Miriam: *(Steps out of her hiding place.)* Boo!

Princess: *(Startled, drops the doll.)* Oh, my!

Miriam: *(Picks up the doll and holds it close.)* I surprised you, didn't I? Anyway, I know a lady who could help you take care of this little baby until he's more fun to play with!

Princess: Great! Just put the bill on my charge card.

Audience: *(Clapping)* Yea!

(Miriam returns to Mom with the doll.)

Mom: Miriam, you're my hero!

Miriam: I think the real praise should go to God. *(Looks up.)* Thank you!

Audience: *(Clasps hands to hearts, looks up.)* Our hero!

If you use this skit as a discussion starter, first read Exodus 2:1-10 aloud, then ask:

● **Why did Moses' mom hide him in a basket?**

● **How did God keep Moses safe?**

● **How does God direct our paths?**

EXODUS 3:1-10

THEME:
God calls us to serve him.

SUMMARY:
With this delightful CRAFT idea, kids learn that God wants us to serve him.

PREPARATION: You'll need green construction paper, glue, and sticky florists' clay. You'll find sticky florists' clay in the craft department of most discount stores. Also provide a clean baby-food jar and a birthday candle for each child. You'll also need a Bible.

Set out the construction paper, glue, florists' clay, and candles.

Hand each child a clean baby-food jar. Show kids how to tear small leaves from the construction paper and glue them to the jar in layers to resemble a bush. For a special touch, consider using various shades of green and yellow paper for the leaves. When each jar is covered with paper leaves, have each child stick a walnut-sized lump of florists' clay in the bottom of the jar. Be sure the clay is centered in each jar. Then help each child stick a candle securely in the clay.

When the "burning bushes" are finished, have volunteers read aloud Exodus 3:1-10. Then ask:

● **What was special about the burning bush?**

● **Who called to Moses from the burning bush?**

● **What did God want Moses to do?**

● **How do you think Moses felt as God talked to him? How would you feel?**

Say: **God called Moses by name. And he calls each of us by our names, too. Just as God had a plan for Moses' life, God has a plan for each of our lives. When you take your candleholders home, set them on the dinner table. Share the story of how God called to Moses from the burning bush. Talk about things God might ask your family to do, then pray together that God will help you be willing to serve him whenever he calls you.**

EXODUS 3:11-12; 4:1-17

THEME:
God helps us when we're afraid.

SUMMARY:
Kids enjoy this unusual DEVOTION that reminds them that with God's help, they'll always say, "I *can!*"

PREPARATION: You'll need duct tape, colored construction paper, plain paper, scissors, markers, and clear tape. You'll also need a clean aluminum can for each child.

Before this activity, collect and rinse out aluminum cans. Cover sharp edges with duct tape. If you have young children, pre-cut three-by-five-inch "labels" from colored construction paper. You'll need one label for each child. You'll also need to cut several small slips of paper for each child.

EXPERIENCE
Set out construction paper, scissors, markers, and clear tape. Keep the small slips of paper to use later. Hand each child an aluminum can. Tell kids to cut paper "labels" to fit around their cans, then write the words: "I can't, but God can!" on the labels. Have older children help younger ones write the words on their labels. Then invite kids to decorate the labels any way they wish. When the labels are finished, have kids tape them around the cans.

Say: **Sometimes we're asked to do things we're not sure we can do.** Ask:

● **Can you tell us about a time when you said, "I can't"?**

Say: **It's easy to say, "I can't." Sometimes we say those words before we've even tried! There was a man in the Bible who kept saying, "I can't" to God. His name was Moses. Let's read what happened when he said, "I can't."**

Have volunteers read aloud Exodus 3:11-12 and 4:1-17.

RESPONSE
● **What was Moses afraid of?**

• How did God help Moses?
• How do you think Moses felt when he understood that God would help him?
• How can God help you this week?

CLOSING

Say: **God wanted Moses to know that with God's powerful help, Moses could do anything. Moses learned that when we can't, God can! You've made cans that say, "I can't, but God can!" Form groups of three or four, and we'll fill our cans with God's power!**

Hand out markers and several slips of paper. Say: **Write or draw a picture of something you're afraid of—something you think you can't do. You don't need to show anyone else what you've written or drawn.**

When kids have finished, say: **Now drop your papers in your God-cans and shout, "I can't, but God can!"** Pause for kids to respond. Then say: **Take your God-cans home. Whenever you're tempted to say, "I can't," write your fear on a piece of paper and drop it in your God-can. Then say, "I can't, but God can!" And remember: God helps us when we're afraid.**

EXODUS 14:13-14, 21-31

THEME:
God saves us.

SUMMARY:
Have kids make this clever CRAFT and part the "sea."

PREPARATION: You'll need cornstarch, water, blue food coloring, cooking oil, clear packing tape, and a plastic one-fourth-cup measuring cup. Also provide a quart-sized, heavy-duty resealable freezer bag for each child. You'll also need a Bible.

Set out the materials, and hand each child a resealable bag. Help each child measure and pour into the bag: one-fourth cup of cornstarch, one-fourth cup of water, and two drops of blue food coloring. Be sure kids remove the excess air from their bags and seal them tightly. Have kids gently knead their bags until the ingredients are completely mixed. Then help each child open the bag and add one-fourth cup of cooking oil. Again have them remove the excess air, reseal the bags, and then knead the bags until the ingredients are smooth and well mixed.

Help each child fold the top edge of the bag down and securely tape the edge to the bag to prevent leakage. Let kids play with the bags. Demonstrate how to lay a bag flat on the table or floor and then run your fingers across the center of the bag to "part" the mixture. Invite kids to try this trick a few times.

Say: **This craft reminds us of a very exciting Bible story. Place your bags in front of you on the floor. I'll read the Bible story while you listen carefully for the part about God parting the sea. When I read that portion of the story, you can part the "waters" in your bags.**

Read aloud Exodus 14:13-14, 21-31. When you get to the part about God parting the Red Sea, allow kids to part the "sea" in their bags. When you're finished, ask:

● **What happened when Moses and God's people came to the Red Sea?**

● **Why did God part the sea?**

● **How has God helped you get across a rough spot in your life?**

Say: **God saves his people because he loves them. God saved Moses and the Israelites from being captured by the Egyptians. He wanted his people safe and sound and far away from wicked Pharaoh. God miraculously parted the Red Sea so his people could get safely across. Take your "sea bags" home and use them to share this story with your families and friends.**

EXODUS 14:13-18

THEME:
God leads and protects us.

SUMMARY:
This fun, interactive SKIT involves the whole class. With the teacher or an older child in the lead, everyone plays Follow the Leader during the story of Moses and the Israelites crossing the Red Sea.

RED SEA, RED SEA, HOW DOES THE CROSSING GO?

SCENE: A Sunday school class acts out the Red Sea crossing with help from the audience.

PROPS: You'll need Bibles for the discussion after the skit.

CHARACTERS:
Teacher
Jeff
Rachel
Sara
Audience

SCRIPT

Jeff: Teacher, tell us the story of the Red Sea crossing,

Teacher: I've told it so often, you want to hear it again?

Rachel: Yes! Start with the part when God speaks to Moses from a burning bush.

Teacher: All right. *(Spoken or sung like the opener for* The Beverly Hillbillies.)*
Let me tell you all a story about a man named Moses.

He was an able shepherd, who had to count a lot of noses.
Then, on a mountain, while watching o'er his lambs,
Out from a burning bush, a voice said, "I Am"!
That was God, you know, King of kings! The Lord of all.

Jeff: What did God tell Moses?

Teacher: God told Moses to tell old Pharaoh to let his people go!

Sara: Why did the people want to go?

Teacher: Because they had been slaves in Egypt for a long time, and they wanted to go home to the land God promised them.

Rachel: How did they go?

Teacher: After Moses showed Pharaoh that God meant business, God's people left. They walked right out of Egypt, toward the Red Sea.

Sara: Can we act it out?

Teacher: OK, let's get in a straight line.

Jeff: *(Points at the Audience, the kids in your class.)* Can they join us?

Teacher: Absolutely! Come on! *(Waits for everyone to get in a straight line.)* Do what I do! Forward march. *(Children march around the room and mimic the Teacher who hops on one foot, walks backward, and walks like a duck.)* Halt! *(Children stop.)*

Jeff: Why are we stopping?

Teacher: The Red Sea is right in front of us!

Sara: But Pharoah's army is coming, we're trapped! Shout for help everyone! *(Everyone shouts, "Help! Help!")* We can't run and we can't hide!

Teacher: *(Pretending to be Moses.)* Pray that God will provide a way.

Rachel: OK, but now what?

Teacher: Hop on one foot. *(Children hop.)* Wait, God didn't say "hop." Let's try again. God says to cross the Red Sea!

Rachel: But we can't swim!

Teacher: Do not fear. *(Waves arms as if holding a staff.)* God will part the waters.

Sara: Wow! The sea is parting.

Teacher: Follow me, gang! Don't fear! God has provided a way! *(All the children march forward except Rachel and Jeff.)* Turn around everyone. See, we've crossed the sea! We're safe on the other side.

Sara: *(Points.)* But look, the army is coming after us. *(Rachel and Jeff gallop angrily, pretending to be the army in hot pursuit.)*

Teacher: Don't fear, God is near! Watch this! *(Rachel and Jeff pretend the waves have collapsed on them.)* Cheer, everyone! *(Everyone cheers, "Yea! Hooray!")*

Teacher: Well gang, God saved the day—again! Let's march back to our seats and thank God for always taking care of us!

If you use this skit as a discussion starter, first read aloud Exodus 14:13-18, then ask:

● **How do you think the Israelites felt when God parted the sea?**

● **When has God helped you with something that seemed impossible?**

• **Why is it important to ask for God's help?**

• **How can you remember to ask for God's help when you're scared?**

EXODUS
16:4, 14-18

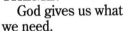

THEME:
God gives us what we need.

SUMMARY:
This edible CRAFT project helps kids get a "taste" for God's divine provision!

PREPARATION: You'll need mini-marshmallows, honey, graham crackers, a large plastic bowl, spoons, a cookie sheet, a microwave oven or electric skillet, and access to a refrigerator. You'll also need a damp towel to wipe sticky fingers. Don't forget Bibles.

Say: **Today we're going to make a mystery treat. I'll need your help.**

Have kids help you pour a bag of minimarshmallows and six tablespoons of honey into a large bowl. Melt the mixture in a microwave oven set on medium. Pause the oven every few seconds, remove the bowl, and let children take turns stirring the mixture until it's smooth. If you don't have access to a microwave oven, you can melt the mixture in an electric skillet, but be sure to supervise the children very closely as they take turns stirring the mixture.

While some children stir the mixture, have others line a cookie sheet with graham cracker halves. Make sure there's a graham cracker half for each child in class. Help children dribble the marshmallow mixture over the graham crackers, then place the "manna" in a refrigerator to chill.

Gather the children in a circle and ask:

• **When you're really, really hungry, what's the first thing you want to eat?**

• **When do you usually feel really hungry?**

Say: **It's not fun to feel hungry. In the Bible, we can read a story about how God provided food for a whole nation of people who were traveling through the wilderness and didn't have anything to eat. We'll read the story aloud and you can help. When you hear what God fed the people, point to your mouths.** Have volunteers read aloud Exodus 16:4, 14-18.

Say: **You look like a flock of hungry little birds!** Ask:

• **What did God feed the Israelites?**

• **If you were a hungry Israelite, what would you say if you saw food raining down from the sky?**

Say: **God knew his people were hungry, so he provided manna for them every day. The people gathered the manna and prepared it to eat. The Bible says that manna looked like thin flakes of frost on the ground. Maybe it looked something like the mystery treat we** made earlier. Let's have a look.

Bring the mystery treat from the refrigerator and say: **Before we eat our make-believe manna, let's say a prayer of thanks for all the food God gives us. Fold your hands.** Pray: **Dear God, thank you for being the perfect provider. We know you give us everything we need, and we give you our thanks. In Jesus' name, amen.**

Let kids enjoy eating the pretend manna, then have them wipe their sticky fingers with a damp towel. You may wish to photocopy the recipe, and send it home so kids can make "manna" for their families.

EXODUS
20:1-17

THEME:
God wants us to obey him.

SUMMARY:
With this MUSIC IDEA, kids enjoy hopping to a rhymin' rap and learn the Ten Commandments in a fun way.

PREPARATION: You'll need a Bible.

Sit in a circle with the kids. Ask:
● **What's one rule you** have at your house?
● **What's one rule you have at school?**
● **What happens when you don't obey those rules?**
● **Why do you think we have rules to follow?**

Say: **There are rules that our government makes up and rules that parents and teachers make up. But God was the first one to give us rules to live by. God gives us rules because he loves us and knows we need rules to help us live safely and get along with others. Let's read about the important rules God gave us. Keep count on your fingers to find out how many rules God gave us.**

Read aloud Exodus 20:1-17. Then ask:
● **How many rules did we just read about?**
● **Can anyone tell us one of the rules?**

Say: **God's ten rules are called the Ten Commandments. The commandments help us live happily and in a healthy way. Let's do a fun rap to learn the Ten Commandments. Stand up and spread out so you have room to move around.**

Lead kids in the following rap. Read the words in rhythm, and encourage kids to bop along with stomping, clapping, or snapping their fingers. Repeat the rap a few times so kids are comfortable with the words. Then review the rap often and before you know it, your kids will be able to recite the Ten Commandments!

THE TEN COMMANDMENT RAP

I am the Lord, your only God.
Don't make false idols—if you hear me, nod.
Don't use the name of the Lord in vain.
Keep the Sabbath holy in sun or rain.
Honor your father and your mother.
You shall not kill your earthly brother!
Stay faithful to that wedding band,
Don't rob or steal, do you understand?
Never tell a lie to the guy next door,
And don't wish to own his boat or car!
If you heard these commandments, hop around,
Turn in place, and then sit down.

EXODUS
20:1-17

THEME:

God gives the Ten Commandments to us.

SUMMARY:

In this SKIT, a TV talk show headlines with Moses, who features God's top-ten countdown. Older children can portray Moses and Dave Bibleman, while younger children will enjoy participating as the Studio Audience.

THE TOP TEN

SCENE: A talk show host interviews Moses.

PROPS: You'll need a flashlight and a piece of cardboard shaped like a stone tablet.

CHARACTERS:
Dave Bibleman
Moses
Studio Audience

SCRIPT

Dave: Hi, welcome to *It's Later Than You Think* featuring me, Dave Bibleman! *(Turns to Studio Audience.)* I need a drumroll here. I'm about to announce the number one top-ten list of all time!

Audience: *(Drums on knees.)*

Dave: Now, I did not write this list, but I have a man sitting next to me who knows who did. Ladies and gentlemen, let's give a very, very big welcome to Moses!

Audience: *(Cheers.)*

Dave: Moses, we're glad you came all the way from Mount Sinai.

Moses: *(Shines hidden flashlight up on his face.)* Thank you, Dave. It's good to be here.

Dave: You seem bright, Moses.

Moses: I've been spending a lot of time with God.

Dave: *(Picks up cardboard tablet.)* Well, it shows. Now tell me, how did you get this top-ten list engraved in stone?

Moses: Well, actually, this tablet was hand-engraved by God.

Dave: Wow! Do you mind if I read this list to the Studio Audience?

Moses: No, go ahead, Dave.

Dave: I'll start from the bottom. Let's see, number ten, "You must not want to take your neighbor's house."

Audience: *(Applauds.)*

Dave: The ninth commandment is "You must not tell lies about your neighbor."

Audience: *(Applauds.)*

Dave: Moses, does this apply to Hollywood gossip writers?

Moses: Absolutely!

Dave: *(Wiggles brows.)* Good. Moving right along. Number eight, "You must not steal."

Audience: *(Applauds.)*

Dave: *(Thoughtfully)* Hmm, would that include borrowing something from a friend and forgetting to take it back...like permanently?

Moses: You've got it, Dave.

Dave: *(Clears throat.)* Top-ten number seven, "You must not be guilty of adultery." *(Looks at Moses)* Does that mean lying to grown-ups?

Audience: *(Applauds.)*

Moses: No, Dave. It means staying true to your husband or wife.

Dave: Mmm...let's see, number six is "You must not murder anyone."

Audience: *(Applauds.)*

Dave: That's pretty clear. Don't kill your neighbor. OK. Number five, "Honor your father and your mother so that you will live a long time in the land."

Moses: Dave, let me point out that's the only commandment that includes a promise from God.

Dave: Cool! It's time for number four, "Remember to keep the Sabbath holy." Moses, what do you think this one is about?

Moses: I think God was telling us to rest on the Sabbath day and

to think about him.

Dave: Now we're at number three, "You must not use the name of the Lord your God thoughtlessly."

Moses: That's right, Dave. We're to only use his name in ways that honor him.

Dave: Can you believe it? We're to number two, "You must not make for yourselves an idol." *(Looks at Moses.)* What do you think God is saying here?

Moses: It's simple, Dave. We're to worship God only—not anything else!

Dave: I get it. Now I need a drumroll for this one.

Audience: *(Makes drumroll.)*

Dave: The number one listing in God's top-ten commandments is "You must not have any other gods except me!" *(Looks excited.)* I get it! God wants us to worship only him!

Moses: That's exactly right, Dave. In fact, I think this whole list can be summed up by saying, "Love the Lord your God with all your heart, and love your neighbor as you love yourself."

Dave: Good review, Moses. *(Turns to audience.)* Let's hear it for the top ten!

Audience: *(Cheers and applauds.)*

If you use this skit as a discussion starter, here are possible questions:

● **How are the commandments meant to help us?**

● **Are the commandments**

good rules for everyone to follow?

Read aloud Exodus 20:1-17. Ask:

● **How can we sum this up?**

● **Which commandment do you think is the easiest to follow? Why?**

● **Which commandment is the hardest to follow? Why?**

EXODUS
25:10-22

THEME:
God is with us all the time.

SUMMARY:
Use this quiet DEVOTION to teach kids that God's presence lights our lives all the time.

PREPARATION: You'll need a medium-sized box, scissors, a sharp nail, aluminum foil, and a powerful flashlight. You'll also need Bibles.

Before this activity, cut a hole in one end of the box for the flashlight to fit through. Then wrap the box with aluminum foil to make it look shiny and special. Poke a sharp nail through the sides of the box to spell the word "God" on each side. When the flashlight is turned on inside the box, the words should light up.

EXPERIENCE

Gather kids in a close circle on the floor, then darken the room as much as possible. Place the box in the center of the circle, and hold the flashlight.

Say: **A long time ago, God told his people to make a special** box to remind them he was with them. They made the box according to God's plan—from special wood covered with gold. On top of the box were angels carved from gold. This box was called the Ark of the Agreement. The box held God's promise to always be with his people. Let's read about this special box.

Have volunteers read aloud Exodus 25:10-22. Then turn the flashlight on in the box so the word "God" lights up on both sides of the box. Say: **The Ark of the Agreement was beautiful, and it helped remind the people of God's presence and light.**

We don't have that special box any longer, but we have God's assurance that he is always with us. If we love God, his love shines in our lives every day.

RESPONSE

Ask:

● **Why don't we need a special box to know that God is with us?**

● **How do you see God's presence shining in your life?**

● **How can you help that light shine in other people's lives?**

CLOSING

Say: **God's love is with us all the time. God is always here, and we don't need a special box to remind us. Let's pray quietly and thank God for his presence in our lives.** Have children pray silently for a few moments. Then end by praying: **Dear God, thank you for being with us every day. Help us shine your love to others so they'll know your presence, too. In Jesus' name, amen.**

LEVITICUS

" 'I am the Lord who brought you out of Egypt to be your God; you must be holy because I am holy.' "

Leviticus 11:45

LEVITICUS 2:11

THEME:
When we show love to others, we're showing love to God.

SUMMARY:
Use this SERVICE PROJECT to help kids express their thanks and love for God.

PREPARATION: You'll need cookies, canned frosting, plastic knives, candy sprinkles, plastic sandwich bags, ribbon, scissors, markers, a large box, and tape. You'll also need a Bible.

Say: Today we're going to have fun making yummy treats to share with another class.

Set out the supplies. Set aside one cookie for each child.

Say: To make our treats, we need to set up an assembly line. One group will be the Spreaders and put frosting on the cookies. The next group will be the Sprinklers and sprinkle colorful decorations on the frosting. Then we'll have the Stuffers put the cookies in bags. The Ribbon Wrappers will tie the bags shut. And the Dazzling Decorators will decorate a box we'll use to deliver our treats. Let's get started!

Let kids volunteer for the various groups. As they work, make encouraging comments such as "You're making such nice gifts to give. When we give to others, we give to God."

When the finished gifts are in the decorated box, gather kids and say: **You worked very hard to make such lovely gifts. God likes it when we show love by doing something nice for others. Let's read what the Bible tells us about giving.**

Read aloud Leviticus 2:11. Say: **The Bible tells us to give back grains without yeast to God. That is just what you've done today. The cookies have no yeast! And when we give to others, we're really giving back to God! Now let's make a second batch of yummy treats. Half of you can be Spreaders and the other half can be Sprinklers. Then you can all be Gobblers!**

If time allows, have kids deliver their cookie-gifts to a class you've arranged to visit.

LEVITICUS 8:10-12

THEME:

We set aside some things as special for God.

SUMMARY:

This CRAFT idea gives kids a special place to pray.

PREPARATION: You'll need a plastic tablecloth, tape, and permanent markers in a variety of colors. Also provide a three-foot square of solid-colored cotton fabric for each child. You'll also need a Bible.

Cover an area of the floor with a plastic tablecloth and tape it in place. Scatter the markers on the tablecloth.

Gather kids near the tablecloth. Ask:

● **What's something you're not allowed to touch or use in your home or at school?**

● **Why do you think that item is so special?**

● **How do you feel if you're allowed to touch something you've never touched before?**

Say: **Some things are set aside because they're special. Maybe your grandma has a special dish or an old quilt she doesn't want anyone to touch. We want to respect those special things and treat them with the best of care. God wants us to set some things aside for him, too. God told Moses to keep some things special and holy, too. Let's find out what those things were.**

Read aloud Leviticus 8:10-12. Then say: **God wanted Moses to sprinkle special oil on certain things. Those things would be holy and special for God. So Moses sprinkled oil on the Holy Tent, the altar, and even his brother Aaron!**

Our prayers are special to God, and he wants us to set aside times to pray. We can make prayer mats to sit or kneel on when we pray. We can keep our prayer mats special for God.

Hand each child a piece of fabric. Invite kids to lay their fabric squares on the tablecloth and decorate the fabric with colorful markers.

When kids are finished decorating their prayer mats, say: **Now** let's sit or kneel on our mats as we say a prayer to God. Pause for children to get settled on their mats. Pray: **Dear God, thank you for the special things you give us. Help us remember to set things aside for you, too. Please help us remember that our prayer time is important and set aside for only you. In Jesus' name, amen.**

Take your prayer mats home and remember to set aside time for God every day!

LEVITICUS 19:1-4, 11-13

THEME:
God gives us rules so we can live strong lives.

SUMMARY:
Use this AFFIRMATION ACTIVITY to help kids see how God's rules make a strong, solid base for our lives.

PREPARATION: You'll need newspaper, clean bricks, and permanent markers. You'll also need a Bible. This activity is best suited for children who can read and write.

Cover a table with newspaper, and set out the markers. Have each child choose a brick and write his or her name on the brick.

Say: **Bricks are strong, and they can remind us of God's rules. God gave rules so we can live strong, happy lives. Let's read about some of God's rules.** Read aloud Leviticus 19:1-4, 11-13, then ask:

● **How can these rules help us live strong lives?**

Say: **Write on your brick one of the rules you just heard.** Pause. **Now pass your bricks to the right. Look at the rule that's already written on the brick you're holding, and add another rule.** Have kids continue this process until the bricks have been passed five times and then returned to their owners.

Say: **God knows that his rules will strengthen our lives. Let's take our bricks and stack them together to see how this works.**

Help kids make a single or double row of bricks, depending on the number of kids in your group. Then say: **God's rules give us a strong base for our lives.** Have kids line up and stand on the bricks.

When everyone is standing on the bricks, say: **Let's give three cheers for God's rules. Hip, hip, hooray! Hip, hip, hooray! Hip, hip, hooray!**

Send the bricks home with the kids to remind them how important it is to live by God's Word.

LEVITICUS
23:39-43

THEME:
We can give thanks to God.

SUMMARY:
This fun OBJECT LESSON helps kids express their thanks to God for his blessings in their lives.

PREPARATION: You'll need scissors; duct tape; and old blankets, sheets, and large towels. You'll also need a Bible.

Place the supplies in the center of the room. Form groups of four and say: **Think about all the good things in your life such as friends, favorite foods, and sunny days to play outside. Let's tell about some of those special blessings.** Encourage kids to each tell about a blessing in their lives.

Say: **God has given us too many blessings to count! We know it's polite to thank people for gifts they give, but did you know that God commands us to thank him? Let's see what God told the Israelites about how they were to thank him for their blessings.**

Read aloud Leviticus 23:39-43. Then ask:

● **How did God want the people to thank him?**

● **What did the people thank God for?**

● **Where did the people live during their festival of thanksgiving?**

Say: **God wanted his people to thank him for the blessings of grain he'd sent during the year. And the people were to live in tents or shelters to remind them how God's people lived in tents when he led them from Egypt. Today we'll build tents of thanksgiving. Each group may choose a few "building materials" from the pile of sheets, towels, and blankets. Work together in your groups to build tents against the walls in the corners of the room. When everyone has built a tent, we'll offer a prayer of thanksgiving to God.**

Circulate and help children build their tents. Show them how to secure the tents to the walls with duct tape. Be sure the tents are large enough to sit in. If you're in an area where there are no walls or corners, let kids drape blankets and sheets over chairs and tables.

When the tents are finished, have kids crawl inside. Stand in the middle of the room so all the kids can hear you, and say: **Let's say a prayer and thank God for his many blessings.** Pray: **Dear God, thank you for all the blessings you give us. We know you love us, and we love you, too. In Jesus' name, amen.**

For extra fun serve small treats, and let the kids eat inside their tents.

NUMBERS

*"So the Israelites moved at
the Lord's command."*

Numbers 9:18a

NUMBERS
3:5-8

THEME:
We all can serve God.

SUMMARY:
As they do this edible CRAFT project, children will discover the joy that comes from serving.

PREPARATION: You'll need napkins, plastic knives, graham crackers, containers of frosting, and paper plates. You'll also need a Bible. Before class, cover tables with newsprint.

Form trios, and give each group napkins, plastic knives, graham crackers, and frosting.

Say: **Let's have fun preparing snacks together. Each group will perform three different jobs. In your group decide who will be a Breaker. Breakers will break the graham crackers into four equal parts. Also choose a Spreader to spread frosting on the crackers and a Stacker to place the crackers together to make graham cracker sandwiches.**

Help kids with their roles. Have the Stackers place the crackers on paper plates. When there are enough cracker treats to feed each trio, gather children and say: **You worked well together to make these great snacks; now you'll need to help each other eat them. Choose a partner from another group, and feed each other a snack. Remember, you** can't use your own hands to eat the snack.

Let kids choose partners and enjoy their snacks. Ask:

● **What was important about each job?**

● **Was it easy or hard to feed someone a snack? Why?**

Read aloud Numbers 3:5-8. Ask:

● **What are some serving jobs in our church?**

● **How can you serve God in church? at home? with your friends?**

Have kids clean up, then say: **You all helped serve in the church today. Sometimes serving is as easy as cleaning up and as much fun as making graham cracker sandwiches. Just as we had different things to do in our trios, God gives us all different jobs to do at church. Every job we do is important when we do it for the Lord.**

NUMBERS
5:5-7

THEME:
God forgives us when we confess our sins.

SUMMARY:
This LEARNING GAME helps kids understand that Jesus paid the price for sin.

PREPARATION: You'll need play money and a Bible. Plan to play this game outside or in a large open area.

Give each child three dollars of play money. Choose two children to be Taggers, and have the rest of the kids scatter around the room. Say: **In this game of Tag, if you're tagged by one of the Taggers, you have to pay a dollar to be set free. If you can't pay a dollar, you have to sit down and be out of the game. Ready? Go!**

Play for a minute or two, then choose two new Taggers. Do not redistribute money between rounds. Gather children together and ask:

● **What was it like to get caught when you had money?**

● **How was it different when you were out of money?**

Read aloud Numbers 5:5-7.

Say: **In our game, you could be free if you had enough money to pay for it. But in life, when we're caught in sin, we have no way to pay for our freedom by ourselves. That's why Jesus died on the cross, to pay the price for our sins. When we believe in Jesus and admit the wrong things we've done, Jesus sets us free from the trap of our sins.**

NUMBERS
9:15-23

THEME:
We can follow God's directions.

SUMMARY:
In this LEARNING GAME, children follow a cloud just as the Israelites did.

PREPARATION: You'll need a sheet of white poster board, scissors, glue, and cotton balls. You'll also need a Bible.

Before playing, cut the white poster board into a cloud shape. Glue cotton balls or scraps of quilt batting onto the poster board to create a fluffy cloud. Clear tables, chairs, and other obstacles from the room.

Read aloud Numbers 9:15-23. Say: **God gave the Israelites a cloud to guide them so they wouldn't get lost in the desert. We're going to follow a cloud while we play a game called Cloud Around.**

Choose a volunteer to hold the cloud and lead the children around the room. Instruct kids to do what the Cloud Carrier does. Encourage the Cloud Carrier to do things such as jump up and down, sing, stomp his or her feet, or twirl in a circle. Have children take turns being the Cloud Carrier and leading the class around the room.

When everyone has had a turn being the Cloud Carrier, have children sit down. Ask:

● **How do you think God's people felt following a cloud? Why?**

● **Why was it important for the Israelites to follow the cloud?**

● **How does God guide us today?**

Say: **God gave us the Bible to help us know what to do. He also listens when we pray and answers our prayers. We can't see him in a cloud, but we know that because God loves us he is always guiding and watching over us.**

Give each child a cotton ball as a reminder that God loves us and leads us every day when we set our hearts to follow him.

NUMBERS 14:1-20

THEME:
God loves us and forgives us.

SUMMARY:
Use this CREATIVE STORY-TELLING activity to teach children about God's love and forgiveness.

Ask:

● **Do you sometimes feel grouchy? When?**

Say: **We're going to have fun with a story that's all about grouchy people and how God loved them and forgave them. Watch me carefully as I tell the story, and do what I do.**

MUMBLERS AND GRUMBLERS

After the Israelites escaped from Pharaoh, they traveled through the desert until they came to the land God had promised them. But in order to live in the land, they would have to drive out the enemies who lived there. They were scared and didn't want to fight, so they grumbled instead. Let's all mumble and grumble the way they did. *(Have everyone mumble and grumble.)*

The Israelites complained to Moses and Aaron. The people didn't want to stay in the desert, but they were afraid to fight for the land God promised to them. The Israelites thought it would be better to go back to Egypt where they had been slaves. But their lives in Egypt had been terrible—they moaned and groaned all the time because of all the hard work they had to do. Let's moan and groan like sad slaves. *(Have kids moan and groan with you.)* But they still wanted to go back. Someone called out, "Let's pick a new leader and go back to Egypt!"

Moses and Aaron got very upset. They bowed down to the ground in front of everyone. *(Have kids put their faces down to the floor.)* Joshua and Caleb tore their clothes to show how sad they were. *(Have kids make a ripping sound.)* They wanted to move into the new land. Joshua and Caleb had seen it when they were spies, so they knew it was beautiful. *(Have children pretend to use binoculars to look over the land.)* There was plenty of food. *(Have kids pretend to eat.)* God would help them, so they didn't have to be afraid.

But the people were so afraid and angry that they thought about throwing rocks at Moses and Aaron and Joshua and Caleb. Then God's glory started shining from the Meeting Tent—the big tent where they worshiped God. *(Have kids shield their eyes.)* It scared all the people. Moses went into the Meeting Tent, and God talked to him. "How long will they not believe me?" God asked. "I will get rid of them. But I will make you into a great nation."

How do you think Moses felt when God said that? *(Pause for response.)* But Moses talked to God *(have everyone get on their knees and fold their hands)*, and God listened. Moses asked God to use his great love *(put hands over heart)* to forgive the people and give them another chance. And God did. Just as God loved and forgave the Israelites, God always loves and forgives us whenever we ask. Let's all give God a great big cheer! *(Have all the kids join you in a rousing cheer.)*

NUMBERS 20:7-12

THEME:
God wants us to obey him.

SUMMARY:
Use this creative PRAYER to help children confess their disobedience.

PREPARATION: You'll need a Bible and a stick.

Form a circle, and have a volunteer read aloud Numbers 20:7-12. Ask:
● What did God tell Moses to do?
● How did Moses disobey God?

Hold up the stick. Say: **We're going to pass this stick around the circle. When the stick comes to you, pound the floor twice like this** (*show children how to bang the bottom of the stick on the floor*), **and think of a time when you've disobeyed. Let's all stay quiet while the stick is passed around.**

Pass the stick to the child on your right. Prompt children each to pound the stick twice as they think of a time when they've disobeyed.

When each child has held the stick, say, **We're going to pass the stick around the circle again. This time instead of pounding the stick, let's all pray, "God help me to obey."** Encourage children to repeat the phrase together as each person receives the stick and holds it.

After everyone has held the stick the second time, hold the stick as you pray: **God, we've all disobeyed and done things that we're sorry for. Thank you for forgiving us whenever we ask. Help us to obey you every day. Amen.**

Have kids all hold onto the stick in the center of the circle as they say a hearty "amen!"

DEUTERONOMY

" 'I am the Lord your God. I brought you out of the land of Egypt where you were slaves. You must not have any other gods except me.' "

Deuteronomy 5:6-7

DEUTERONOMY 1:19-33

THEME:
God is bigger than our fears.

SUMMARY:
During this TRIP to a museum, children realize that God is bigger than their fears.

PREPARATION: Two weeks before your field trip, go to a local natural history museum or zoo to find large animals or replicas of them. Arrange for parents to drive groups of children to the museum or zoo. Recruit one adult helper for every five children. You'll need a Bible and an instant-print camera for the trip.

Take children to a natural history museum or zoo. Let children stand near replicas of large, ferocious animals. If you go to a zoo, be sure to visit exhibits such as the lions, polar bears, and tigers. Using an instant-print camera, take pictures of kids while they stand next to (but at a safe distance from!) the biggest, scariest creatures they can find. As children walk through the museum or zoo, talk about the big, scary things we face in life. Then gather the class at a picnic spot nearby, and ask children to tell about their biggest fears. You may want to start the discussion by telling about things that frighten you or things that frightened you when you were a child.

Tell children that God's special people, the Israelites, faced lots of scary things when they prepared to enter the land God promised them. Have a volunteer read aloud Deuteronomy 1:19-33.

Explain that God was sad that his people didn't trust him with their fears. Distribute the pictures you took on your field trip. Have kids hold their pictures as they pray, thanking God for being bigger than their fears.

DEUTERONOMY 1:21-33

THEME:
We can trust God.

SUMMARY:
This fun, interactive SKIT involves everyone in a twist on the story of the twelve spies.

GET SMART—TRUST GOD

SCENE: Spies return with reports for Israel.

PROPS: You'll need a broom and small footstool. Make a giant grape cluster from circles of purple construction paper or by blowing up blue or purple balloons and tying them together.

CHARACTERS:
Aaron
Caleb
Joshua
Moses
Spy 1
Spy 2
Spy 3
Israelites

SCRIPT
Special instructions: Kids who don't have an assigned part can be the Israelites. Instruct them to cheer when Spy 3 gives a thumbs up signal and to boo when Spy 3 gives a thumbs down.

Aaron: *(Shields eyes and points.)* Hey, Moses, take a look. Could those be our spies returning?
Moses: *(Shields eyes.)* It could be...it might be...
Aaron: It is!
Spy 3: *(Gives thumb up.)*
Israelites: Yea!
(Joshua, Caleb, and all the spies enter as a group. Spies 1 and 2 carry a broom across their shoulders with a giant cluster of grapes hanging from the broom.)
Caleb: Agent Caleb reporting, sir.
Aaron: Well, let's have it!
Joshua: Wait until you see the land God has promised us. It's grrr-eat!
Caleb: Agent Joshua's right. It's good. *(Pretends to pluck a grape and eat it.)* Mmm! That's really good. It must be a land of milk and honey!
Joshua: And grapes!
Moses: *(Claps his hands.)* How wonderful!
Spy 3: *(Gives thumb up.)*
Israelites: Yea!
Spy 1: Aren't you forgetting something, Caleb?
Caleb: What do you mean?
Spy 1: *(Stands on footstool.)* Listen, people! The land is filled with giants. If we try to march in there, they'll mow us down like grasshoppers!
Spy 3: *(Gives thumbs down.)*
Israelites: Boo!

Joshua: Wait, I think you're the ones who are forgetting something. As I recall, God is the one who told us to take the land.

Spy 2: All I know is, those guys are bigger than Godzilla! Whoever tries to take that land will die.

Spy 3: *(Gives thumbs down.)*

Israelites: Boo!

Caleb: *(Stands on footstool.)* Listen, my friends. Don't let these spineless spies feed you sour grapes! Get smart—trust God. God will win the battle for us.

Spy 3: *(Gives thumbs down.)*

Israelites: Boo! *(Scene freezes.)*

Joshua: *(Steps out of scene, walking like an old man.)* Well, here we are forty years later, Caleb.

Caleb: *(Steps out to join his friend. Has also aged.)* It looks like it's up to us to lead our people into the Promised Land.

Joshua: Too bad their parents would not listen to *(points up reverently)* THE CHIEF forty years ago.

Caleb: I know *(shaking his head)*, instead they died in the desert.

Joshua: *(Puts his arm around Caleb.)* I guess we'll show those giants a thing or two, at last.

Caleb: You bet we will! With God on our side, we have nothing to fear!

Spy 3: *(Steps out of frozen scene, gives thumbs up.)*

Israelites: Yea!

Permission to photocopy this skit from *The Children's Worker's Encyclopedia of Bible-Teaching Ideas: Old Testament* granted for local church use. Copyright © Group Publishing, Inc., P.O. Box 481, Loveland, CO 80539.

If you use this skit as a discussion starter, here are possible questions:

● **Why wouldn't the people take the land that God had promised them?**

● **What happened to them when they disobeyed?**

● **When is it hard for you to trust God?**

● **How can we encourage each other to trust God?**

DEUTERONOMY 6:4-9

THEME:
God wants us to love him and remember his commands.

SUMMARY:
In this wearable CRAFT project, children create reminders of God's love and special rules.

PREPARATION: You'll need scissors, a package of blue cold-water fabric dye, a bucket, and an old white sheet or pillowcase. You'll also need a Bible, permanent markers, rubber bands, and a clothesline.

Before this activity, cut the sheet or pillowcase into strips that are three-by-twenty-four inches long. You'll need one strip for each child. Mix the fabric dye in a bucket, according to package directions. Plan to do this activity outside, and encourage kids to wear old clothes.

Read aloud Deuteronomy 6:4-9. Say: **This verse says to tie**

God's commands to our foreheads. That means that God wants us to make him and his special rules the most important things in our lives. In Bible times, people sometimes wore special bands called phylacteries (fil-LACK-tur-ees) around their foreheads and arms to remind them of God's laws. Let's have some fun making our own special headbands.

Give each child a strip of fabric, a permanent marker, and ten small rubber bands. Have kids write, "Love the Lord your God" in the center of their strips.

Then say: **I'm going to read the Ten Commandments from Deuteronomy 5:6-21. After each commandment, I'll pause while you twist a rubber band tightly around your headband. You'll want to space the ten rubber bands evenly down the length of your headband.**

When you've read the Ten Commandments, and kids have their rubber bands wrapped tightly, help kids take turns dipping their headbands into the dye. Encourage kids to be careful not to splash the dye. Lay the dyed headbands in the sun to dry. You may want to let kids take their damp headbands home in plastic sandwich bags.

Say: **When your headbands are dry and you take off the rubber bands, you'll discover a fun, tie-dyed pattern. Plus, you'll have a great reminder to keep God first in your life!**

You may want to encourage kids to wear their headbands the next time you meet.

DEUTERONOMY 8:1-10

THEME:
Obey God's commands.

SUMMARY:
Play this LEARNING GAME to help kids understand the importance of listening and obedience.

PREPARATION: You'll need newsprint, string, scissors, blindfolds, a Bible, and a minidoughnut for each child. Tie a twelve-inch length of string to each doughnut.

Form trios, and give each group a sheet of newsprint. Say: **In this game you'll receive a tasty treat if you listen closely and obey my instructions. First, decide who will be the Taster, the Teacher, and the Twister in your group.** When trio members have chosen their roles, instruct them to place the newsprint on the floor.

Say: **The object of the game is to eat your entire doughnut.** Give a doughnut-on-a-string to each group member. **If you're a Taster, sit cross-legged on the newsprint. If you're a Twister, you'll hold the doughnut-on-a-string for the Taster. But first the Twisters need one more thing.** Distribute blindfolds, and help the Twisters put them on. **The Twisters will need the Teachers' help to know how to get the doughnuts into the Tasters' mouths. You'll have one minute to help your Taster eat a doughnut. When I call time, trade places. We'll play until each** person has had a turn eating a doughnut.

Say "go," and let kids begin. After one minute, say "stop," and have kids trade roles. Repeat the game two more times so each person has a chance to eat a doughnut. Then form a circle and ask:

● **What was it like to catch a twisting, twirling doughnut?**

● **How did it feel to feed someone without seeing them?**

● **What kinds of instructions were helpful?**

Read aloud Deuteronomy 8:1-10. Ask:

● **What special instructions does God give us?**

● **What happens when we obey?**

Say: **God gives us special rules and directions because he loves us. Just like the Teacher in our game, God can see the whole picture, so he knows what's best for us. God wants to give us blessings we can sink our teeth into! When we listen to God and obey his commands, we'll get to "taste" his blessings!**

DEUTERONOMY
28:1-14

THEME:
God blesses us when we obey him.

SUMMARY:
Use this AFFIRMATION ACTIVITY to help kids share blessings with each other.

PREPARATION: You'll need a Bible and balloons.

Say: **A blessing is something that comes from the Lord.** I'm going to read a passage from the Bible that tells about lots of different kinds of blessings. Listen carefully and see if you can count the number of blessings in this passage. Here we go.

Read aloud Deuteronomy 28:1-14, then ask children to name some of the blessings they heard.

Say: **The Lord does all kinds of good things for us! But did you know that we can give blessings to each other? When we say something good about a person, that counts as a blessing. Let's see how it feels when we bless each other.**

Form groups of no more than five, and have each group form a circle. If you have fewer than ten children, form one group. Ask one volunteer from each group to sit in the center of each circle. Give each person a balloon.

Say: **Think of something good to say to the person in the middle of your circle. You might say something like "You show God's love," "I like your smile," or "God has good plans for you." If you're sitting in the middle, blow a puff of air into your balloon each time someone blesses you. Tie off your balloon when it's full.**

Older children may need to help younger ones blow up and tie off their balloons. When each person has a full balloon, say: **Your blessings filled up each other's balloons!** Ask:

● **How did the blessings fill**

you up on the inside?
• **How do God's blessings fill up our lives?**

Pray together and thank God for all his blessings.

JOSHUA

" 'Always remember what is written in the Book of Teachings. Study it day and night to be sure to obey everything that is written there. If you do this, you will be wise and successful in everything.' "

Joshua 1:8

JOSHUA 1:5-9

THEME:
Be strong in the Lord.

SUMMARY:
Use this PARTY IDEA to reinforce children's budding bravery and strength in the Lord.

PREPARATION: Several weeks before the party, send out invitations shaped like barbells. Write, "Be Strong and Brave" on the center bar and party information on the weights at the ends. You'll need party supplies as described below for the activities you choose to do.

Throw a "Heroes of the Faith" party to encourage children to be strong in the Lord. To set the atmosphere, play theme music from *Rocky* or *Chariots of Fire* or Michael W. Smith's "Be Strong and Courageous."

Set up a snack table with healthy, strength-building snacks, such as carrots and celery sticks, peanut butter, pretzels, melon balls, and juice. Also set out small plates, cups, napkins, and toothpicks. Challenge kids to use the ingredients to build their own "tower of strength" food sculptures. Then let kids devour their towers!

Have children form groups and make "comic strip stories" of the following Bible heroes: Joshua (Joshua 3:1–4:24); Gideon (Judges 7:1-22); David (1 Samuel 17:1-50);

Abigail (1 Samuel 25:1-35); Esther (Esther 2:2-18; 3:1–5:8; 7:1-10); and Daniel (Daniel 6:1-28). Give each group the name of a Bible hero, the Bible reference where that hero's story is found, a long strip of shelf paper, and markers. Have groups share their finished comic strip stories with the entire group.

Make "barbells" by taping black balloons to the ends of wrapping-paper tubes painted black. Have an instant-print camera handy, and snap a picture of each child lifting the "heavy" barbells.

Let kids create an obstacle course using tables, chairs, inner tubes, scraps of lumber, a clothesline, and anything else you have on hand. Have kids form pairs. Have one partner wear a blindfold as the other partner guides him or her through the obstacle course. Then have partners trade roles. Compare relying on partners to relying on God. Explain that because God is all-powerful, when we trust in him we can always be strong and courageous.

JOSHUA
2:2-21

THEME:
God keeps his promises.

SUMMARY:
In this CRAFT project, kids will make red-rope reminders to help them remember that God keeps his promises.

PREPARATION: You'll need a Bible, red fabric, and craft beads.

Cut the fabric into one-inch strips the width of the fabric.

Before this activity, make a sample red-rope reminder from the instructions below, and hang it in a window or on a door.

Say: **I'm going to read you a Bible story about spies, a woman who helped them, and a secret signal. When you think you know what the secret signal is, clap your hands one time.**

Read aloud the story of Rahab and the spies from Joshua 2:2-21. Then ask:

● **What was the secret signal?**
Ask:

● **Do you think the spies kept their promise to Rahab?**

Say: **Let's find out what happened.** Read Joshua 6:23. **The spies did keep their promise to Rahab. They destroyed the whole city, but saved all of Rahab's family. Just as Rahab could count on the spies to keep their promise, we can count on God to keep his promises. Let's make red-rope reminders so we can remember that God keeps his promises.**

Hold up the sample red rope you made, then give each child three strips of red cloth. Tell children how many beads they can choose, then show them how to tie the three cloth strips together at one end and braid the three strips. Have them add beads to their red ropes anywhere they'd like—simply by slipping a bead onto the strip that's in the middle of the braid. To finish, have each child tie a knot at the end of the braid.

Say: **You can choose how to**

use your red-rope reminder. You may want to hang it in your window as Rahab did, or hang it on your bed, or wear it as a headband. Each time you see it, remember that God keeps his promises.

JOSHUA 4:1-9

THEME:
It's important to remember what God has done in our lives.

SUMMARY:
Use this art and CRAFT project to help kids create reminders of all God has done for them.

PREPARATION: You'll need acrylic craft paint, paintbrushes, wiggly eyes, glue, and one rock for each child. You'll also need a Bible.

Have volunteers read Joshua 4:1-9. Ask:
● **Why did God want the men to collect rocks?**
● **What was special about the rocks?**
Say: **The rocks that the men picked up came from the middle of the river. Normally it would be impossible to get to those rocks because they were under the water. But God had stopped the flow of the river so all the Israelites could cross safely. Joshua took the river rocks and piled them up to mark the place the Israelites crossed the river.**

Every time God's people looked at that pile of river rocks, they would remember that God had helped them cross the river on dry ground.

Let's make our own special pet rocks. As you take care of your pet rocks, they can remind you that God takes care of you every day just as he took care of the Israelites.

Set out the supplies. Have each child choose a rock. Invite kids to decorate the rocks to look like silly creatures. As kids work, encourage them to tell about times when God has taken care of them. Close by praying: **God, thank you for taking care of us every day. Help us to trust you just as the Israelites trusted you when they crossed the river. Amen.**

JOSHUA 6:1-20

THEME:
God's power is great!

SUMMARY:
In this active DEVOTION, children act out the story of the battle of Jericho and learn that God is more powerful than our problems.

PREPARATION: You'll need Bibles, empty cardboard tubes, old sheets, permanent markers, and masking tape.

EXPERIENCE
Form two groups, and have

them sit on opposite sides of the room. Explain that Group 1 is the Israelites and Group 2 is the Walls of Jericho. Distribute the Bibles, and have groups take turns reading aloud Joshua 6:1-20.

Give Group 1 cardboard tubes and markers. Instruct the kids to make "trumpets" by decorating the cardboard tubes.

Hand out the old sheets and additional markers to Group 2. Encourage the kids to draw large stones on the sheets to make them look like the walls of a city.

When the groups are finished decorating, have the Walls stand up and hold their sheets around them. Instruct the Israelites to form a line and march around the Walls. You may want to have them sing "Joshua Fit de Battle of Jericho" while they march. Tell children to pretend that it's the seventh day in the story and to count out loud as they march around the Walls seven times blowing their trumpets. When they complete the final time around, have them shout. Then signal the Walls to fall down.

Let groups trade roles and repeat the enactment.

RESPONSE
Ask:
● **How do you think the Israelites felt while they marched around the walls?**
● **How did they see God's power on the seventh day?**
● **When have you seen God's power in your life?**

Attach the "wall sheets" to a wall in your classroom. Have kids use markers to draw or write their fears, frustrations, and problems on the

wall sheets.

CLOSING
Say: **The Israelites might have been afraid of the people in the mighty, walled city of Jericho. But when they followed God's instructions, they saw that he was more powerful than anything.** Point to the wall sheets. **God is more powerful than our problems, too. Let's shout and watch them fall down.**

Lead children in shouting, then pull the sheets off the wall.

JOSHUA 7:1-20a

THEME:
We can't keep secrets from God.

SUMMARY:
In this QUIET REFLECTION, children see how secret sins aren't a secret from God.

PREPARATION: You'll need a colorful throw rug or blanket, paper, pencils, and a large trash can with a lid. You'll also need a Bible.

Place the throw rug on the floor in the center of the room. Distribute the pencils and sheets of paper. Ask kids to write down something they've done wrong, such as lying, stealing, disobeying, or being unkind. Nonreaders may draw pictures. Reassure children that no one will see what they've drawn or written. Then have kids wad up their papers and put them under the throw rug. Invite kids to sit in a circle around the rug. Read aloud Joshua 7:1-20a.

Say: **We all have secret sins that we haven't told anyone about. Achan took something he wasn't supposed to and then tried to keep it a secret. But it showed up just like all these bumps under the rug.** Ask:

● **Who was hurt by Achan's secret sins?**

● **When you keep a sin secret, who gets hurt?**

● **What does God want us to do when we do something wrong?**

Scoop up the paper wads, and wrap them in the rug. Open the large trash can, shake the paper wads into it, and put the lid back on. Say: **Hiding our sins doesn't make them go away. Only God can remove our sins and get rid of them. When God forgives our sins, he puts a lid on them, and we don't have to keep feeling bad about them. We're completely forgiven. Let's ask God to forgive us for the sins we wrote down.**

Give children a few moments to pray silently, then close with a short prayer of thanks for God's forgiveness.

JOSHUA 24:14-15

THEME:
God wants us to choose him.

SUMMARY:
Use this LEARNING GAME to reinforce and encourage each child to put God first.

PREPARATION: You'll need markers, scrap paper, a large trash can, a clothesline, and a Bible.

Have a volunteer read aloud Joshua 24:14-15. Say: **In Joshua's time a lot of people made fake gods of wood and stone.** Ask:

● **How do you think it would feel to bow and pray before a statue made of wood or stone?**

Say: **We don't worship fake gods today, but sometimes we pay too much attention to things that aren't really important. Sometimes those things can push God into last place in our lives.** Ask:

● **What kinds of things keep you from putting God first in your life?** Encourage kids to mention things such as TV, sports, toys, and friends.

Set out markers and scrap paper. Ask children to draw at least three pictures of the things that tempt them and use too much of their time. Explain that the pictures will be used for a game and won't be kept. Ask kids to wad their finished pictures into paper balls.

Place the large trash can in the

center of the room. Lay a ten-foot clothesline circle around the trash can. Invite kids to stand around the circle and shoot "baskets" with their paper wads. Each time someone "scores," have all the kids shout, "Choose God!" Play until all the paper wads are in the trash can.

Have kids join hands around the circle. Pray: **Dear God, we want to choose you today. We're throwing away things that tempt us to forget you. Help us remember that you're our one, true God. In Jesus' name, amen.**

JUDGES

*"The angel of the Lord appeared to
Gideon and said, 'The Lord is with you,
mighty warrior!' "*

Judges 6:12

JUDGES
2:16-19

THEME:
God wants us to obey the
authorities.

SUMMARY:
On this field TRIP, children discover the importance of knowing and obeying the authorities.

PREPARATION: You'll need a
Bible. Arrange for a trip to a local
police station or ask an officer to
visit your group. Let the officer
know that you want the children to
understand that police enforce the
law and help people stay safe.

Have kids listen as the officer
explains about his or her job.
Be sure to let children ask questions. Have the police officer
explain what might happen if people were allowed to do whatever
they wanted, such as drive too fast
or take things from a store.

After meeting with the officer,
explain that God gave judges to
the Israelites to keep them safe.
Have volunteers read aloud Judges
2:16-19. Ask:

● **What did the judges do?
What did the people do?**

● **Why do we need police
officers and judges?**

● **How can we stay safe?**

Say: **We can stay safe and
please God by obeying the law.
God gives us police officers,
judges, parents, and teachers to**

protect us and keep us safe. Remember that police officers can't be everywhere, watching people all the time, but God *is* everywhere and always watches over us.

JUDGES 6:11-16

THEME:
Through God's great power, we can do amazing things.

SUMMARY:
Use this OBJECT LESSON to help kids realize that God's power helps us do his will.

PREPARATION: For every two children, you'll need a Bible, a potato, and a drinking straw.

Form pairs, and give each pair a Bible, a potato, and a drinking straw. Have partners read Judges 6:11-16 together. Then say: **God asked Gideon to do something very hard. Let's see if you can do something tricky! Take turns trying to poke your straw into the potato.** Allow a few moments for pairs to try this. Then say: **God knew that Gideon couldn't do the task on his own. But with God's power behind him, Gideon could do anything! I think you need some power behind you, too.**

Show children how to cover one end of the straw with a thumb. When they poke the straws into the potatoes, the air pressure will stiffen the straws, and the straws will go right in!

Say: **Tell your partner one task you need God's help with— maybe it's learning to do an acrobatic trick, making friends with someone who doesn't seem to like you, getting on a sports team, or learning to play a musical instrument.**

Allow time for partners to share. Then have kids form a tight circle and pile their hands together in the center of the circle. Say a brief prayer asking God's help and power. Then have kids shout, "Go in God's power!" and break the pile of hands on the word "power."

JUDGES 6:33-40

THEME:
God knows the future.

SUMMARY:
Through this LEARNING GAME, kids understand that we can't predict what will happen but that God knows everything.

PREPARATION: You'll need paper, pencils, a Bible, and small wrapped candies.

Have kids sit in a circle. Say: **We're going to play a guessing game. I'm going to hide a candy in one of my hands. Then I want you to guess which hand the candy is in.** Hold your hands in front of you, and put the candy in one hand. Make it obvious so the children plainly see which hand you've put the candy in. Ask:

● Where is the candy hidden?

● How did you know that?

Say: It was easy to find the candy when you saw me put it in my hand. What will happen if I. put my hands behind my back when I hide the candy?

Put your hands behind your back, and slip the candy into one hand. Bring your closed hands back out in front of you, and let the children choose which hand they think is holding the candy. Then form pairs, and give each pair two candies, a sheet of paper, and a pencil. Say: Take turns hiding a piece of candy from your partner just as I did the second time. You'll each get three turns. Write down how many times you guess correctly. After a minute, ask:

● How many of you were able to guess correctly all three times?

● What would have made it easier?

Have volunteers read aloud Judges 6:33-40. Say: Gideon wanted to know for sure that God was going to help the Israelites win in their battle against Midian. Ask:

● How do you think Gideon felt when he asked God for a sign?

● Can you think of a time when you wanted to know what was going to happen next?

Say: When you played the guessing game, you didn't *know* where the candy was—you could only guess. We don't know for sure what will happen to us, but we can trust that God has us in his hands! When we trust God, we don't have to guess about our future—we know it'll be sweet!

Allow kids to enjoy their candy treats.

JUDGES
7:1-22

THEME:

God's power helps us do hard things.

SUMMARY:

In this CREATIVE STORYTELLING activity, children journey with Gideon as he chooses his men for battle.

Before telling this story, go over the following cue words and actions with the children. Encourage them to listen closely for the cue words and do the accompanying motions.

● Gideon—Fold hands in prayer.

● drink—Pretend to drink.

● trumpet—Blow a pretend trumpet.

● Lord—Raise a fist, and say "yes!"

A TEENY, TINY ARMY

Long ago the Israelites lived close to the Midianites, who were their enemies. The <u>Lord</u> promised <u>Gideon</u> that the

Israelites would beat the Midianites in a big battle. So Gideon got an army ready. He had thirty-two thousand men. That was a pretty big army! But the Lord said to Gideon, "You have too many men." The Lord didn't want the Israelites to brag about how they could win on their own. He wanted them to trust in him.

So the Lord told Gideon to let everyone go home who felt afraid. Twenty-two thousand men left; ten thousand stayed. Gideon thought that was OK. He still had a big army. But the Lord thought the army was too big. He told Gideon to have the men get a drink of water from the river—the Lord would choose men for the army by the way they got a drink.

The men who got down on their knees to drink were sent away. The Lord chose three hundred men who got a drink by using their hands to bring water to their mouths, lapping it as a dog does. Only three hundred men. That was a teeny, tiny army! How would they ever fight the big, strong Midianites?

The Lord let Gideon go near the camp of Midian. Gideon overheard two Midianite soldiers talking. One soldier had dreamed about Gideon and the Israelites winning the battle. So Gideon went back to tell the three hundred men that the Lord had prepared a victory for them.

Gideon gave each man an empty jar, a torch, and a trumpet. On his signal, the men were to break the jars, hold the torch-es high, and blow the trumpets. The Lord would win the battle for them. When the trumpets sounded, the Midianites began fighting each other. Then they got scared and ran away! Gideon and the three hundred men stood on the hills around the camp. The Lord had won the battle!

JUDGES 16:4-22

THEME:
Temptation takes us away from God.

SUMMARY:
Use this active DEVOTION to help kids learn about temptation and discover ways to defeat it.

PREPARATION: You'll need blankets, wrapped candies, string, scissors, paper, pencil, and a watch with a second hand. You'll also need a Bible.

In a large room, arrange the furniture and blankets to form a maze. Create at least three "forks" in the maze that require the kids to choose a path. Make one of the paths for each fork a dead end. Scatter the wrapped candies at the beginning of each dead end.

EXPERIENCE
Say: **We're going to hear a story about the world's strongest man who got caught in a trap.** Have volunteers read aloud Judges 16:4-22. Say: **Samson got twisted**

up in temptation. He made some wrong turns that caused him a lot of trouble. We're going to try twisting and turning in this maze. Each of you will get two chances to go through the maze. The object is to complete the maze as quickly as possible. I'll time you to see if you can beat your first time.

Let children take turns going through the maze. Record their times.

RESPONSE

After each child has tried the maze twice, have children sit in a circle. Ask:

● **What made it easier the second time through the maze?**

● **How many times did you stop the first time?**

● **What made you want to stop the first time?**

Say: **The candy might have tempted you to turn toward it, but each time it led to a dead end.** Ask:

● **How was Samson tempted in the Bible story?**

● **What did Samson do?**

● **What are some things that you feel tempted to do?**

Say: **We all feel tempted sometimes. When your parents say it's time for bed, you might be tempted to pout or get angry. When your teacher blows the whistle to end recess, you might be tempted to pretend you didn't hear it. Temptation only leads to dead ends. The real treat is to follow Jesus.**

CLOSING

Distribute the candies from the maze. Pray: **Dear God, help us to trust you every day. Keep us away from temptation, and let us do what you want. Let these pieces of candy remind us that temptation is a dead end, and you are the sweetest treat in the world! Amen.**

JUDGES
16:4-31

THEME:
God wants us to walk away from temptation.

SUMMARY:
This interactive SKIT is great for all ages. Have an older child portray Samson, who leads the group in some crazy Samson exercises.

PUMP IT UP!

SCENE: Samson leads an exercise video.

PROPS: You'll need a roll of toilet paper, a curling iron, a pair of blunt scissors, and a swimming cap or stocking. Also provide a cassette or CD player and a cassette or CD of jazzy aerobic music. For the discussion following the skit, you'll need a Bible.

CHARACTERS:
Samson
Delilah
three Strong Men
Group
Column 1
Column 2

SCRIPT

Special instructions: Play jazzy music whenever Samson is exercising. For added fun use a video recorder so kids can watch, learn, and laugh again and again!

Samson: Hello, all. *(Shows off his muscles.)* Welcome to PUMP IT UP! As you know, you're all here today to be in my new exercise video. I want all of you to start with one thousand jumping jacks! OK, let's start! Up, down, up, down... *(Group joins him in jumping jacks.)*

Delilah: *(Interrupts.)* Oh, Samson, it's time for our first commercial.

Samson: *(Stops and shows his muscles.)* Now for a word from our sponsor.

Delilah: Today Samson's going to share the secret behind his strength.

Samson: *(Shows biceps.)* Darling, you know that's a secret between me and God.

Delilah: *(Flirty)* Oh please, Samson. Do it for me.

Samson: All right. If you wrap me in strong new ropes, I'll be weak as a baby.

Delilah: Isn't that a coincidence? Our sponsor this break is the Strong New Rope Company. Let's show 'em boys.

Strong Men: *(Run out and wrap Samson in toilet paper.)*

Samson: *(Laughs.)* Stop! That tickles! All right, gang, back to our exercises. Let's do a thousand reps of "swing that jawbone." *(As he swings his arms, the toilet paper falls to pieces.)* One, two, three, four, one, two, three, four... *(The Group exer-*

cises with him.)

Delilah: *(Flirty)* Oh, Samson, you're too funny. You told me a little fib.

Samson: *(Stops exercising.)* You know how much I love to tease you, honey pie.

Delilah: *(Pouty)* I know. But I really want to know the secret of your strength. Won't you please tell me?

Samson: All right, lamby, curl my hair, and ZAP the power goes right out of me.

Delilah: How lucky—our next sponsor is Curly's Curling Irons. Here, let me try one on you. *(Pretends to curl a lock of his hair.)*

Samson: *(Hops up and shows his muscles.)* All right. It's time to catch those foxes! Lean, reach, grab. Lean, reach, grab. Lean, reach, grab... *(The Group exercises with him.)*

Delilah: *(Stamps her foot!)* Why, Samson, you lied to me again! How can I ever trust you?

Samson: *(Stops.)* Do I really have to tell you my secret, sweetie?

Delilah: I wish you would, then I'd know you really loved me.

Samson: *(Sighs deeply.)* All right, the secret of my strength is my hair. If I ever cut it, I'll be weak as a kitten, kitten!

Delilah: Is that a fact, love? Well, our next sponsor is the Sharp Scissors Company.

Strong Men: *(Run to Samson and PRETEND to cut his hair. While they do this, Samson puts a swimming cap or stocking over his head to look as if he's bald.)*

Samson: AUGGG! *(Falls to the floor.)* I'm weak as a baby!

Delilah: *(Happily)* YES! *(The Strong Men drag him away.)* Samson was captured that day by his enemies. Many years later his enemies were at a big party. Samson was invited, too, so his enemies could laugh at him. Samson was blind and asked his guards if they would place him between two columns. *(Samson uncovers his hair.)* No one noticed how long Samson's hair had grown!

Samson: *(Stands between Column 1 and Column 2.)* Lord, hear my prayer: Give me strength to destroy my enemies today. *(Samson pushes against the Columns, and they fall down. Samson sighs and falls down too.)*

Delilah: The secret of Samson's strength was not really in his hair; it was in his God. And that day, God gave him the strength to bring the roof down on all the enemies of his people. And on that day, the enemy and Samson were no more.

If you use this skit as a discussion starter, read aloud Judges 16:4-31, then ask:

● **What was Samson's mistake?**

● **If you were Samson's friend, what advice would you have given him about Delilah?**

● **When have you felt tempted to do something wrong?**

● **What's the best way to escape from temptation?**

Ruth

" Where you go, I will go. Where you live, I will live. Your people will be my people, and your God will be my God.' "

Ruth 1:16b

RUTH 1:3-18

THEME:
Friends are faithful.

SUMMARY:
In this LEARNING GAME, partners try to stick together while circumstances try to pull them apart.

PREPARATION: You'll need a Bible.

Form two groups, and send them to opposite sides of the room. Have Group 1 form two lines facing each other, about five feet apart. Tell kids that this is the Tunnel of Troubles, and they are the Trouble-makers. Instruct members of Group 2 to find partners to be their Best Buddies. Have the Best Buddies link arms and then line up at one end of the Tunnel of Troubles.

Say: **These Buddies will try to walk through the Tunnel of Troubles without being pulled apart. Each Troublemaker in the Tunnel may use two fingers of one hand to try to pull the Buddies apart. Troublemakers, be careful not to poke or scratch—just tug with two fingers. If you succeed in pulling the Best Buddies apart, they'll join your group. Ready? Go!**

Send the first pair of Best Buddies through the tunnel. Remind the Troublemakers to be gentle as they play. When all the Best Buddies have had a turn, have groups trade roles and play again. Following the game, have groups exchange high fives, then invite everyone to sit in a circle. Ask:

● **What made it hard to go through the tunnel?**

● **What kinds of troubles pull real friends apart?**

Read aloud Ruth 1:3-18. Ask:

● **What made Ruth a faithful friend?**

● **How can you be a faithful friend?**

Have kids form one big circle and sing the chorus of a song such as "Friends."

RUTH
2:8-20

THEME:
God loves to see kindness in action.

SUMMARY:
Through this SERVICE PROJECT, kids experience giving kindness to those who need it.

PREPARATION: Check your local paper to find out when your community puts on a Special Olympics for people with disabilities.

Have a group of kids sign up to volunteer at a Special Olympics festival in your area. Older children can time events and measure jumps, while younger children can pass out water and give encouraging pats on the back.

Before the Special Olympics, gather kids in a circle. Have a volunteer read aloud Ruth 2:8-20.

Ask:

● **Who showed kindness to Ruth? What did he do?**

● **Why do you think Boaz chose to be kind to Ruth?**

● **Who does God expect us to be kind to?**

● **How can we show kindness as we help today?**

When you return to the church, gather kids and discuss the following questions:

● **What was it like to help the athletes?**

● **What's the difference between helping these young people and any other young people?**

● **Why did these athletes need your kindness?**

● **What did you learn from volunteering today?**

This service project not only meets a need for the Special Olympics but may help your children better understand people who are different.

RUTH
3:10-15

THEME:
Caring for others shows our love.

SUMMARY:
Through this OBJECT LESSON, kids realize the importance of taking care of those around us.

PREPARATION: You'll need to bring in a gentle pet, such as a puppy, a cat, a hamster, or a rabbit.

Form a circle, and have children sit down. Say: **I've brought a special guest to our class today. When I bring our guest in, please stay seated and be quiet and gentle.** Bring in your "guest" animal, and introduce it to the kids. Then say: **Taking care of an animal is lots of work. I'll bring** (name of pet) **around to let each of you pet it. As you do, tell one thing a person needs to do to care for a pet.**

When each child has had a turn to pet the animal and share, have an adult helper take the animal outside or return it to its cage. Ask:

● **What would happen to an animal if you didn't take care of it?**

● **How is caring for a person different from the way we might care for a pet?**

● **Why is it so important to take care of those around us?**

Say: **Listen as I read how Boaz took care of Ruth. Then turn to a partner, and tell one way you can take care of someone the way Boaz did.**

Read aloud Ruth 3:10-15. When children have finished sharing, say: **Now find two or three other people, and tell them one way you'll take care of your family and friends this week.**

RUTH
4:14-22

THEME:
God has great plans for us.

SUMMARY:
Plan a Fabulous Future PARTY to show kids the wonderful plans God has in store for them.

PREPARATION: Make posters and fliers to advertise a Fabulous Future party. Decorate your party room with streamers and balloons. Gather supplies for the activities you choose to do. You'll need a Bible for the devotion at the end of the party.

Invite kids to a Fabulous Future party to celebrate all the possibilities God has for them. Form teams and play Charades. Have kids pantomime things they'd like to do in the future, such as driving, hang gliding, or building a house.

On index cards have kids write silly predictions, such as "You'll invent chocolate sneakers, and kids everywhere will elect you president" or "You'll set the world record for the number of marshmallows you fit in your mouth." Tape the cards to a wall, face down. Have kids take turns tossing suction cup darts at the cards, then reading their "futures" aloud.

Set up a portrait studio with wacky dress-up clothes and an instant-print camera. Allow children to dress up as grown-ups of the future and take each other's pictures.

Set out a variety of snack foods, such as pretzels, marshmallow creme, graham crackers, cheese spread, peanuts, raisins, and M&M's. Challenge kids to create foods of the future—snacks that will be popular ten or fifteen years from now. Have kids vote on their favorite snack creations. Bring several different flavors of presweetened drink mix. Let kids combine different flavors to create their own wild taste sensations.

Wind up the party with a devotional time. Ask a volunteer to read aloud Ruth 4:14-22. Ask:

● **Why do you think Ruth and Boaz ended up with such a bright future?**

● **How does God direct our future?**

● **Is our future up to God or up to us?**

● **What's one thing you wish for your future?**

Close with a brief prayer, thanking God for filling us with so many possibilities.

1 SAMUEL

" 'God does not see the same way people do.
People look at the outside of a person, but the
Lord looks at the heart.' "

1 Samuel 16:7b

1 SAMUEL 1:24-28

THEME:
God wants us to give our best.

SUMMARY:
This active DEVOTION helps children want to give God their best.

PREPARATION: Before this activity, place over-ripe bananas in gift boxes, and wrap the boxes with shiny paper. You'll need one gift box for every two children. (After the activity, you can use the bananas to make banana bread at home.) You'll also need pencils, bowls, plastic knives and spoons, good bananas, ice cream, and your choice of toppings to make banana splits. And don't forget a Bible.

EXPERIENCE
Form pairs, and distribute the gift boxes. Say: **I've brought a beautiful gift for each of you today. I hope these gifts will show you how much I care for you. That's why I wrapped them in such pretty wrapping paper. Go ahead and open them.** When children open their gifts, allow them to express disgust or surprise.

RESPONSE
Keep the bananas out on the floor and ask:
● **What did you think of your beautiful gifts?**
● **Did I give you my best?**

● What would be the best gift I could give you?

Have volunteers take turns reading aloud 1 Samuel 1:24-28, then ask:

● What did Hannah give to God?

● Do you think she gave God her best? Why or why not?

Say: **When Hannah gave her son, Samuel, to God, she was giving God the best thing she had. Hannah wanted to show God how much she loved him.** Ask:

● What can you give to show God you love him?

CLOSING

Say: **Wrapping up mushy bananas in pretty paper didn't make them better gifts. It's important to give God the best of our time, money, talents, and life.** Distribute the pencils. **On a scrap of wrapping paper, write down the three best things you have that you'll give to God this week.**

Encourage kids to keep their lists and refer to them during the week.

Then say: **Just to show how much I really do care for you, I have some nicer bananas. I also have ice cream and toppings. Let's make banana splits!**

1 SAMUEL 3:4-10

THEME:
God helps get us ready to serve.

SUMMARY:
In this LEARNING GAME, kids feel the excitement of getting ready to serve the Lord.

PREPARATION: You'll need a Bible and wrapped candies.

Stand near one wall of the room, and have kids line up at the opposite wall. Say: **As I read the following story, listen for the word "lead." It's the word that's in the saying, "You can lead a horse to water, but you can't make him drink." When I say "lead," take two giant steps toward me. The first person to touch the wall behind me will get a prize. But remember, you can only move when you hear the word "lead." If you move at the wrong time, take two steps backward. Listen carefully!"**

TEACHER TIP
If your room is small, make arrangements to use a larger room for this activity. If the weather is nice, you may want to take kids outside.

Read the following story slowly, drawing out the underlined words to make children anxious to move.

Once there was a boy named Lee who loved to rake leaves.

Lee would rake the leaves into a huge pile, lean his rake against the tree and leap into the pile. Sometimes Lee would even lead his dog, Levi, on his leash, walking around the neighborhood and picking up leaves. Then he'd lead Levi to the baseball park, where he would show off his treasures. Well, Lee's love of leaves soon caught on. Before long, all the kids in Little League were collecting, raking, and, at least, jumping into piles of leaves. Lee would lead his friends on great expeditions into the forest, where they would see who could find the biggest leaf. Lee was always in the lead!

Reward the child who touched the wall first or came the closest with a treat. Then say: **I think you all deserve a treat!** Toss handfuls of wrapped candies in the air until each child has one. Gather kids in a circle and ask:

● **What were you thinking of as you listened to the story?**

● **Why were you so excited to move ahead?**

Read aloud Samuel 3:4-10, then ask:

● **How were you like Samuel in this game?**

● **How can you show God that you're ready to serve him?**

Say: Samuel was the same age as many of you when God spoke to him, and he went on to be a great prophet and leader of God's people. You don't need to wait until you're older to serve God—you just need to be willing to listen. I believe that God can do great things through you just as he did through Samuel!

1 SAMUEL 16:7

THEME:
God sees our inner beauty.

SUMMARY:
Through this AFFIRMATION ACTIVITY, kids discover that God looks at their hearts.

PREPARATION: Before this activity, cut out a five-inch cardboard heart for each child in your class. Wrap each heart in aluminum foil to make it look like a mirror. You'll also need a pad of sticky notes, pencils, and a Bible. This activity works best for older kids who can read and write.

Distribute the foil-covered hearts and say: **Look at yourself in your mirror. Tell me what you see.** Allow a few kids to respond. **When we look at ourselves or at other people, we tend to see just what's on the outside. Let's find out how God looks at us.**

Have a volunteer read aloud 1 Samuel 16:7. Then ask:

● **How does God see us?**

● **Are you glad God sees what we're like on the inside? Why or why not?**

Say: **People spend lots of time trying to make themselves look good on the outside, but it's what's on the inside that counts!** Ask:

● **How can we get beautiful on the inside?**

Say: **We can't make ourselves**

beautiful on the inside, no matter how hard we try. But God can! When we ask God to fill our hearts with his love, God takes away all our sins and bad feelings. Let's take a couple of minutes to look at each other the way God looks at us.

Give each student a pencil and six small sticky notes. Have kids write good qualities they see in the people on each side of them. Then have children put their sticky notes on their neighbors' mirrors. Close by saying: **As you read these special notes, remember that this is the way God sees you—from the inside out!**

1 SAMUEL
17:17-50

THEME:
God is our helper.

SUMMARY:
Use this David and Goliath SKIT for children in third through sixth grades. Kids act out scenes from David's life while David convinces King Saul to allow him to face Goliath.

THE GIANT MEETS A ROCK

SCENE: David comes to Israel's camp and defeats Goliath.

PROPS: You'll need an adult full-length coat and a strong nonfolding chair. You'll also need to make a harp, a sword, and a slingshot from cardboard.

CHARACTERS:
David
Eliab
Giant
Guard 1
Guard 2
Guard 3
King Saul
Lion
Bear

SCRIPT

David: *(Strums cardboard harp and sings to the tune of "Heigh-Ho" from* Snow White.*)* Heigh-ho, heigh-ho, it's off to camp I go—to bring some mail and wish them well, heigh-ho, heigh-ho . . .

Eliab: *(In hiding)* Who goes there?

David: It is I, David the shepherd boy, coming to bring my brothers chocolate chip cookies and news from home.

Eliab: Little bro! *(Hugs him.)* How's the family?

David: Fine, Eliab. *(Wiggles eyebrows.)* Cindy Lou says hi.

Eliab: *(Digs his foot in the ground and looks bashful.)* Aw shucks, tell her hi, too.

David: What's the news at camp? Are we beating the Philistines?

Eliab: No, the battle isn't going well. In fact, it's not going at all. It seems we have a little . . . well really . . . a BIG problem.

David: What's too big for God?

Eliab: It's almost time . . . you'll see.

Giant: *(Standing on chair, wearing the long coat that covers the chair, adding to appearance of height. Holds the large cardboard sword. Shouts in deep voice.)* Fe fi fo fum! I smell the blood of a Hebrew man. If he can fight me, let him come. Fe fi fo fum!

David: So who's going to fight him?

Guard 1: *(Quakes.)* Not I.

Guard 2: *(Pops out of nowhere.)* Not I.

Guard 3: *(Pops out of nowhere.)* Not I.

David: Then I will do it myself! Take me to the king!

Eliab: *(Shrugs.)* He'll never allow it, David. You're too little. *(Takes David to King Saul.)*

King: So you want to fight the giant Goliath. But you're only a kid! Did you see the size of that giant? He's one mean fighting machine.

David: *(Stands at attention.)* I know I'm just a kid, sir. I keep my father's sheep. But with God's help...

Lion: Roar! *(Springs at David, and David kills him.)*

David: I have killed a lion...

Bear: Growl! *(Stands on his hind legs and attacks David. David kills him.)*

David: And a bear. *(Wipes the sweat off his brow.)* If I can kill a lion and a bear, with God's help I can kill that giant!

King: Here's my armor and sword!

David: *(Tries to lift the sword, but it's too heavy. Pulls slingshot out of his pocket.)* Thanks, king. But If you don't mind, I'll use this instead.

Giant: *(In a deep voice)* Fe fi fo fum! I smell the blood of a Hebrew man. If he can fight me, let him come. Fe fi fo fum! I'm waiting! *(Taunting)* Are you men or are you mice?

David: *(Pretends to pick up stones.)* Prepare to die, Goliath!

Giant: Ha, ha, ha! Why if it isn't a tot with an itty-bitty slingshot! *(Grinds his fist into his palm.)* I'll make mincemeat out of you, boy!

David: *(Shouts.)* You come to me using a sword and two spears, but I come to you in the name of the Lord All-Powerful, the God of the armies of Israel! The battle is the Lord's!

Giant: *(Taunting)* Na—na, na-na-na!

David: *(Pretends to shoot stone at giant.)*

Giant: *(Grabs forehead, jumps off chair, staggers a few steps, and falls down.)*

David: *(Raises arms in victory.)* The victory is the Lord's!

If you use this skit as a discussion starter, read aloud 1 Samuel 17:17-50, then ask the following questions:

● **Why wouldn't the soldiers in the army of Israel fight the giant?**

● **Why was David willing to face the giant?**

● **What's a giant problem you have faced?**

● **How did God help you?**

1 SAMUEL
17:45-49

THEME:
With God, we can do anything.

SUMMARY:
Take a field TRIP to help kids discover that God can take away their fears and frustrations.

PREPARATION: Find a tall tree or building within a block of your meeting area. Get permission to write on the tree or building with chalk. Then make at least one water balloon for each child, and put the balloons in a laundry basket near the tree. Bring a Bible with you for the Scripture reading.

In your classroom, say to the students: **I have a special surprise field trip planned for you today. On our way, I'm going to tell you about a young man who conquered a scary enemy. Let's go!** Lead children toward the location where you placed the water balloons. Carry the chalk and Bible with you. Tell this story as you go.

Long ago there lived a boy named David. David was the youngest of eight brothers. He had the lowest job of anyone in the family—it was his job to watch the sheep. His older brothers became soldiers and went off to fight the Philistines—how exciting! But David had to watch the sheep day after day after day. Can you show me what a flock of sheep would sound like?

One day David's father told him to go to the battlefield and take his brothers some food. David was excited. Finally he would get to see the battlefield! So David gathered up a bag of food and set off for the battlefield.

When he arrived, David found his people, the Israelites, trembling before a giant named Goliath. Goliath was mocking the Israelites, saying that they were afraid of him. That made David angry! "Why does he think he can speak against the armies of the living God?" David asked. But everyone was too afraid of Goliath to fight him. Let's think of some things that we're afraid of.

When you arrive at the tree or wall you've chosen, distribute the chalk, and allow kids to write or draw things that are scary to them. When everyone has drawn or written at least one thing, collect the chalk, and continue the story:

The only person who wasn't afraid of Goliath was David. So David talked to the king and persuaded the king to let him fight the giant. Instead of fighting with a sword, David decided to use the weapon he always used as he watched over the sheep—a sling. As Goliath looked on, David gathered five smooth stones from a nearby stream and put them into his bag.

We'll pretend that these water balloons are our stones. Distribute the water balloons. **Let's read from the Bible what David said to Goliath.** Have a volunteer read aloud 1 Samuel 17:45-47. Say: **Then David took a stone from his bag,**

placed it in his sling, and slung it! Toss your water balloons at those scary things just as David slung the stone.

Clap as the water from the balloons cleans away the chalk, then continue with the story:

The stone hit Goliath in the forehead, and he fell down. David won the battle! A little shepherd boy defeated the meanest giant in the land! Ask:

● Why did David have more courage than the soldiers?

● When do you feel brave?

● Can God help you the way he helped David? Explain.

Say: Look at the scary things you wrote about and drew. Some of them are totally gone; others are faded or running. With God's help, we can be as brave as David and put our fears on the run!

1 SAMUEL 18:1-4

THEME:
Friendship is a gift from God.

SUMMARY:
In this wearable CRAFT activity, kids make friendship bracelets to give away.

PREPARATION: You'll need safety pins and several different colors of embroidery floss. Cut the floss into sixteen-inch lengths, but do not separate the six smaller strands. Make a sample bracelet ahead of time to

show the children. You'll also need a Bible.

Read aloud 1 Samuel 18:1-4. Ask:
● What gifts did Jonathan give David?

● Why do you think Jonathan gave David such special gifts?

Say: Jonathan's gifts showed how much he cared for David. Let's make friendship bracelets to give to our friends.

Let each child choose four different colors of floss. Demonstrate how to hold the ends of the strands together and tie a knot with a two- to three-inch tail.

Then instruct each child to sit on the floor and use a safety pin to anchor the knotted end to his or her sock or a rug. Lead children through the following steps to make their bracelets.

1. Choose a color to start with and pull it to the right, and hold it in your right hand. Gather the other three strands in your left hand.

2. Loop the starter strand under the group of three strands and pull it away from you to make a tight knot at the top. Repeat this process eight times, making sure that each successive knot is flush with the

previous one.

3. Choose another color, and repeat the above process. Be sure to use all three of the other strands before using the first color again. Continue until the bracelet fits comfortably around a wrist or ankle.

4. Gather all the strands together and tie them off, leaving a two- to three-inch tail for tying. Remove the safety pin.

Encourage kids to give their bracelets to a special friend.

2 SAMUEL

"He [David] said: 'The Lord is my rock, my protection, my Savior.'"

2 Samuel 22:2

2 SAMUEL 6:1-5, 14-15

THEME:
God enjoys celebration and worship.

SUMMARY:
In this MUSIC IDEA activity, children form groups and create new ways to celebrate with praise music.

PREPARATION: Select an upbeat worship song that celebrates God, such as "How Majestic Is Your Name" or "What a Mighty God We Serve." Bring in a cassette or CD player and a copy of the song. You'll also need a Bible.

Say: When David defeated the Philistines, he led the Israelites in a great celebration. Let's read about David's worship celebration, then plan a worship celebration of our own.

Have volunteers read aloud 2 Samuel 6:1-5, 14-15. Ask:
● Why were the Israelites celebrating and worshiping God?
● What can we celebrate and worship God for?

Form three groups—the Motion Makers, the Crazy Clappers, and the Cheerleaders. Explain that you're going to play a song, and each group will come up with a way to celebrate along with the music. The Motion Makers will make up unique actions, the Crazy Clappers will create exciting clapping rhythms, and the Cheerleaders will come up with a list of things they can celebrate such as God's goodness, power, creation, or love.

Once kids understand their roles, play the song. Then allow about five minutes for groups to come up with their celebration elements. Play the song again, and have the Motion Makers teach their motions, the Crazy Clappers lead their clapping rhythms, and the Cheerleaders shout out their reasons to celebrate.

2 SAMUEL
9:6-13

THEME:
Kindness helps us grow.

SUMMARY:
In this QUIET REFLECTION, children remember those who have shown them kindness.

PREPARATION: In the middle of the room, set up a table of delicious treats or a simple meal. Make the table as attractive as possible, with nice silverware, plates, and candles. You'll need a Bible for the Scripture reading.

Say: **After Saul and Jonathan died, King David showed great kindness to Jonathan's son, Mephibosheth** (me-FIB-o-sheth). **Let's read about David's kindness.** Have a volunteer read aloud 2 Samuel 9:6-13. Ask:

● **What kind things did David do for Mephibosheth?**

● **Why do think David did such kind things?**

Have kids stand about ten feet away from the table you've prepared. Say: **It was a great privilege for Mephibosheth to eat at the king's table. Today I'd like you to think about people who've been especially kind to you. I'll name some special times or situations and give you a moment to think of someone who was kind to you. Then you can take a step toward our "king's table."**

Encourage children to be quiet as you read the following list. Pause between each item to allow time for kids to think of someone who was kind to them.

● **Think of someone who was kind to you when you were in a new place.**

● **Think of someone who was kind to you at school.**

● **Think of someone who was kind to you at church.**

● **Think of someone who was kind to you when you were afraid.**

● **Think of someone who was kind to you when you didn't expect it.**

When everyone is standing at the table, say: **Now think of one person you can be kind to.** Pause. **Think of one place you can be kind to that person.** Pause. **Before we enjoy our feast, let's pray, asking God to help us show kindness to others.** Lead children in prayer, then let them enjoy their treats at the king's table.

2 SAMUEL 22:1-4

THEME:
Prayer and praise please God.

SUMMARY:
In this PRAYER and praise activity, kids offer "pop-up prayers" of thanksgiving.

PREPARATION: You'll need a bucket and several handfuls of buttons or coins. You'll also need a Bible.

Place a bucket on the floor. Have kids form a circle around it, several feet away from the bucket. Have a volunteer read aloud 2 Samuel 22:1-4.

Say: **David wrote a song to praise God. We have lots of reasons to praise God too. Let's show our thanks to God with pop-up prayers. Think of things you'd like to thank God for. When you've thought of something, shout it out as you pop a button into the bucket. You can pop up a button any time— even while other kids are. We'll keep popping and shouting our thanks until we've used up all the buttons.**

Drop a few buttons into each child's hands. Have kids continue thanking God until they run out of buttons. Close by giving God a standing ovation.

2 SAMUEL 24:20-25

THEME:
God rewards our sacrifices.

SUMMARY:
Use this active DEVOTION to help children understand what it means to sacrifice.

PREPARATION: Before this activity, make paper money by writing, "friends," "education," "money," "health," and "time" on slips of green paper. Make enough money so each child has three of each type of "dollar bill." If you have several younger children in your group, pair them up with older children who can help them with the money. You'll also need pencils and a Bible.

EXPERIENCE

Distribute the paper money so each student has three of each type of bill. Then say: **I've just given each of you a handful of money. Each dollar is valuable. You can use the dollars to purchase different things. I'll read a list of ways you can spend your money. When I read the price for each item, decide whether or not you want to pay the price for that item. If you do, come up and pay me.**

Read the following list, and allow kids to decide if they're willing to pay the price for each item.

● **Your new group of friends would be impressed if you went in-line skating without a helmet and knee pads. The price tag to go in-line skating this way is two** health dollars.

● Your family has volunteered at a soup kitchen for a Saturday afternoon. The price tag for your Saturday afternoon is three time dollars.

● Your friends want to ditch school and sneak to a movie. The price tag for ditching is two education dollars.

● A visiting missionary needs money to help sick children in another country. The price tag to help the missionary is three money dollars.

● You and a friend stole a toy from a department store. When you tell your mom what you've done, both you and your friend get into trouble. The price tag for honesty is one friend dollar.

Before continuing, make sure each child has at least one of each type of bill. Pass out additional dollars if necessary.

RESPONSE

Ask:

● What made an item worth paying the price for?

● What are some consequences of paying the price?

Say: Let's find out the price King David paid to show his love for God. Read aloud 2 Samuel 24:20-25. Then ask:

● What did David give to show his love to God?

● Why didn't David take anything from Araunah (a-RAW-nah)?

● What made it worth the price?

CLOSING

Say: We can give our time, money, friends, or belongings to show God how much we love him. Distribute the pencils. On the back of each dollar, write one way you can give something to show how much you love God.

When children finish, close in prayer, expressing your love to God. Encourage children to take their money home as a reminder of their commitment to give.

1 KINGS

" 'Obey the Lord your God. Follow him by obeying his demands, his commands, his laws, and his rules that are written in the teachings of Moses. If you do these things, you will be successful in all you do and wherever you go.' "

1 Kings 2:3

1 KINGS 2:2-4

THEME:
Following God is a wonderful journey.

SUMMARY:
Take kids on a field TRIP to help them realize that following God leads to wonderful rewards.

PREPARATION: Choose a recreational spot for a class picnic. Pack treats, drinks, and a Bible in a picnic basket. Place the basket at your picnic site—at the end of the hiking trail, in the shade near a bike path, or under a tree at a nearby park. Have a teen or adult helper stay with your basket of goodies until your group arrives.

Take kids to a park, desert, or mountain area where there are hiking, biking, or walking trails. Be mysterious about where you're headed; just lead kids along the way without telling them your destination. Continue your walk for several minutes, then lead children to the basket of goodies. As kids enjoy the treats, read aloud 1 Kings 2:2-4. Ask:

● **Why did you follow me even though I didn't tell you where we were going or why we were going there?**

● **How was following me on this hike like following God?**

● **What kinds of rewards come when we follow God?**

● **What encourages you to**

follow God faithfully?

Close with a prayer of thanks for God's faithfulness and guidance in our lives.

1 KINGS
3:4-15

THEME:

God helps us make wise choices.

SUMMARY:

At this PARTY, kids learn the importance of making wise decisions.

PREPARATION: Send out invitations to "A Party of Choices." Decorate your meeting room with festive streamers and balloons. Provide healthy snacks, such as vegetables and dip, fruit kabobs, crackers, cheese, and juice. You'll also need supplies for the activities you choose that are explained below.

As kids arrive, tape a card with the name of a Bible character on each child's back. Choose Bible characters who made either wise or foolish decisions. Wise characters might include Noah, Moses, Ruth, Solomon, Esther, or Mary. For foolish characters you might choose Eve, Lot's wife, Haman, Jonah, Judas, or Peter. On the back of each card, write a simple summary of the wise or foolish decision that person made. To guess their characters, have kids ask each other questions that have simple yes or no answers.

Set up boxes that are labeled "1," "2," and "3." Play a simple trivia game, letting each child who gives a correct answer choose one of the boxes. Put different prizes under the boxes for each round of play. Be sure some prizes are silly, such as a box of bandages or a pair of old shoelaces. Good prizes could include quarters, treats, pencils, or balls. Encourage kids to shout "Wise choice!" when someone selects a good prize or "Silly choice!" when someone selects a silly prize.

Have kids count off by twos and form two teams. Then let each team choose a leader to be at the front of a train. Have kids form two trains by lining up and holding onto the waists of those in front of them. Blindfold the leader of one train. Then instruct both leaders to take their teams on a two-minute train ride around the room. To debrief, have kids sit in a circle and discuss the importance of choosing good leaders as they grow up.

Have kids sit in a circle. Distribute markers and paper. Say: **If you could choose to have one thing in all the world, what would you choose? On your paper, draw or write what you would choose. Don't sign your name on the paper, and don't let anyone else see what you draw or write.** When kids have finished, collect and shuffle the papers. Display them one by one, and have kids guess whose paper you're displaying. Then say: **In Old Testament times, God actually gave this choice to a king named Solomon. Let's read about what Solomon chose.** Read aloud 1 Kings 3:4-15. Ask:

● **What other things might King Solomon have asked for?**

● **Why do you think he chose wisdom?**

● **Do you think Solomon's choice was a good one? Why or why not?**

Close with a prayer asking God to help kids make good choices.

1 KINGS 3:16-28

THEME:

God wants us to ask for wisdom.

SUMMARY:

In this SKIT, kids of all ages get involved as wax figures come to life in a story about Solomon's wisdom.

WAXING WISDOM

SCENE: Kids visit a museum where they discover wax figures that tell a story about Solomon's wisdom.

PROPS: You'll need a baby doll and a cardboard or plastic sword.

CHARACTERS:
Linsey (museum curator)
King Solomon (wax figure)
Mom 1 (wax figure)
Mom 2 (wax figure)
Guard (wax figure)
Group

SCRIPT

Special instructions: Cue the wax figures to move whenever Linsey isn't looking. Instruct the Group to laugh each time the wax figures move.

Linsey: *(To the Group)* Welcome to the Museum of Bible History. I'm your tour guide, Linsey Tells-All. Please walk this way *(walks, swinging one leg to the side)* to look at our wax figures depicting wisdom. *(Group, also swinging legs, follows Linsey to frozen actors portraying scene of two women holding a baby, kneeling before King Solomon. A "frozen" Guard with a big sword is standing by the King.)*

Linsey: See how life-like King Solomon looks as he sits on his throne. This was one wise king. Once God told him he could have whatever he wanted, and King Solomon chose wisdom instead of riches. *(Linsey turns her back on the display to talk to the Group.)*

King: *(When Linsey's back is turned, King Solomon comes to life and waves at the Group.)*

Group: *(Laughs.)*

Linsey: *(Turns and looks at figures, who freeze.)* I don't see what's so funny about that! Anyway, you're all probably familiar with the story about the two women who came to Solomon because they were having a fight over a baby.

Moms 1 and 2: *(When Linsey's back is turned the two women come to life and begin to play Tug of War with the baby doll.)*

Group: *(Laughs.)*

Linsey: Honestly, people, this is a serious story! Anyway, both women claimed to be the mother of the baby. They wanted Solomon to settle their argument. Wise Solomon said the baby should be cut in half with a sword.

Guard: *(The guard with a sword poses to cut the baby in two.)*

Linsey: *(Not noticing)* King Solomon was wise. He knew the real mother would stop him. She did. *(Wax figures act out Linsey's story as her back is turned.)* The real mother told King Solomon to spare the child and to give it to the other woman. That's when King Solomon knew which woman was really the baby's mother.

King: *(Acts as if he has just thought of a bright idea. Stands up and gives the baby to the real mom.)*

Group: *(Applauds and cheers.)*

Linsey: Honestly, children, you act as if this display came to life. *(When Linsey turns her back the wax figures take a bow.)*

If you use this skit as a discussion starter, here are possible questions:

● **How is wisdom better than riches?**

● **What should you do if you want wisdom?**

Read aloud 1 Kings 3:16-28. Ask:

● **How did the king know which woman was the mother of the baby?**

● **How did Solomon's decision show that he was wise?**

1 KINGS 11:7-13

THEME:
There's only one true God.

SUMMARY:
In this CRAFT project, kids celebrate ways to describe our one true God.

PREPARATION: You'll need markers, index cards, Bibles, and large sheets of newsprint. On each index card write all of the following Scripture references: Psalm 23:1; Psalm 28:1; Psalm 42:11; Psalm 43:2; Isaiah 1:24; John 6:45; 1 Timothy 6:15; James 1:17; Revelation 1:8; and Revelation 15:3.

Say: **King Solomon of Israel was famous for his wisdom. But as he grew older and richer, Solomon did some things that weren't wise at all. Let's read about one of Solomon's unwise and sinful actions.** Have a volunteer read aloud 1 Kings 11:7-13. Then ask:

● **What did Solomon do wrong?**

Say: **The Bible teaches us that there is only one God and that we worship only him. Let's make special banners to remind us how wonderful our one true God is.**

Form groups of three to five. Give each group markers, a Bible, a sheet of newsprint, and an index card with the Scripture references written on it.

On the newsprint, instruct kids

to write, "The Only 1," making the "1" a large outline that fills most of the paper. Have volunteers in each group look up the Scripture passages. Have kids work together to fill in the hollow "1" with words from the passages that describe God. Kids might write words such as "Shepherd," "Rock," and "Savior." As kids work, you might want to play songs such as "Great Is the Lord" and "We Will Glorify." Then have kids display the banners around the room as reminders that our God is the one true God.

1 KINGS
17:2-16

THEME:
God takes care of us.

SUMMARY:
In this creative PRAYER, kids thank God for all that he provides.

PREPARATION: You'll need pencils, slips of paper, and a Bible. This activity requires writing, so pair any younger children in your group with a partner who can write.

Say: **Today we're going to hear about the very unusual ways God took care of a man and a woman. Boys, listen for the way God took care of the man. Girls, listen for the way God took care of the woman.**

Read aloud 1 Kings 17:2-16. Then ask:

● **Boys, how did God take care of the man?**

● **Girls, how did God take care of the woman?**

● **How does God take care of you?**

Have kids form trios. Give each trio pencils and several slips of paper. Have kids write on the slips of paper things that God provides for them, such as food, shelter, clothing, friends, a church, family, and sunshine. When kids have written on all their slips, have them divide the slips among the trio members and then form a circle with the whole class. Have kids hold their slips in their open palms.

Pray: **Lord, thank you for all the good things that come from your hand. Thank you for showering us with your blessings every day.** Then have children toss the slips of paper in the air as they shout, "Thank you, God!" Have kids scoop up the slips of paper on the floor and toss them again. Keep the "shower of blessings" going for at least thirty seconds.

1 KINGS
18:18-39

THEME:
God is powerful.

SUMMARY:
In this CREATIVE STORYTELLING activity, kids act out the story of Elijah and the prophets of Baal.

PREPARATION: Before class, build an altar of blocks. Distribute a few flashlights, and have kids hide them under their shirts or behind their backs until you give them a signal near the end of the story.

WHY BOTHER WITH BAAL?

Once there was a prophet named Elijah who loved and followed God. Unfortunately, the king of Elijah's country did not love and follow God. King Ahab was wicked—he worshiped an idol called Baal. King Ahab was so bad that we're going to boo when we hear his name. God was angry that Ahab *(Boo!)* worshiped Baal, so God didn't send any rain to King Ahab's *(Boo!)* land. The drought dried up all the rivers, creeks, and streams. Even the grass and cattle were dying.

So God sent Elijah to see King Ahab *(Boo!)* and tell him to stop worshiping Baal so the drought would end. Elijah told Ahab *(Boo!)* to gather all the people of Israel at Mount Carmel and to make sure the 450 prophets of Baal came, too. Elijah chal-lenged the prophets of Baal to a showdown!

Everyone gathered at Mount Carmel. Let's gather at our altar of blocks. *(Lead children to the altar that you built.)* The 450 prophets of Baal prepared meat for a sacrifice, then prayed to their fake god and asked him to set the meat on fire. They shouted and begged and danced and carried on all day, but nothing happened. The fake god Baal couldn't answer their prayers.

Finally it was Elijah's turn. He dug a ditch around the altar and said, "Fill four jars with water, and pour it on the meat and on the wood." Then he had the people pour water again and again! The wood got soaked. The water ran off the altar and filled the ditch. While all of Israel watched, Elijah prayed, "Lord, you are the God of Abraham, Isaac, and Israel. Prove that you are the God of Israel and that I am your servant." Then fire from the Lord came and burned up the sacrifice, the wood *(motion for the children with the flashlights to shine them on the altar)*, the stones, and the ground around the altar. It even dried up the water in the ditch!

The people of Israel stopped worshiping Baal and believed in the one true God. And that very day rain began to fall again. King Ahab's *(Boo!)* fake god Baal had been defeated. God Almighty had won!

1 KINGS
19:11-13a

THEME:
God is with us.

SUMMARY:
In this SKIT, kids learn about Elijah listening for the voice of God. The activity works best with third graders and up.

THE GOD SQUAD

SCENE: Elijah is visited by detectives.

PROPS: You'll need a pen and note pad, a toy detective badge, and a death-threat note. For the Scripture reading, you'll need a Bible.

CHARACTERS:
Joe Friday
Sergeant Saturday
Sergeant Sunday
Elijah
Group

SCRIPT

Group: *(Hums Dragnet theme. Friday, Saturday, and Sunday enter stage.)*

Friday: *(Speaks in monotone.)* The time is 3 p.m. It's a sunny Tuesday afternoon here in Judea. Sergeants Saturday and Sunday are here to help me follow up on a rumor. We've gotten a tip that the prophet Elijah heard God's voice. My name is Friday, Joe Friday. *(Turns and knocks on imaginary door.)*

Elijah: *(Opens door.)* Yes?

Friday: Hi, I'm detective Joe Friday with the Judean God Squad. *(Flips out his badge. Nods to other detectives who are standing with him.)* These are my partners Saturday and Sunday. We're here to ask you a few questions, Elijah.

Elijah: What do you want to know?

Friday: What were you doing forty-two days ago?

Elijah: I was running for my life, why?

Saturday: *(Scribbles on pad.)* Who was pursuing you?

Elijah: Wicked Queen Jezebel. She was pretty mad when God dropped fire on my altar, and her fake god Baal left her altar without a spark.

Sunday: Was this a contest of some kind?

Elijah: You could say that. We wanted to see who was real— her god or mine. Mine won.

Friday: Is that why you were running for your life?

Elijah: *(Pulls note out of his pocket.)* You could say that. Queen Jezebel sent me this death threat.

Friday: *(Reading)* "I'll kill you, Elijah!" *(Looks up.)* Why do you suppose Jezebel threatened you?

Elijah: After my God defeated her fake god, the people killed her priests. She blamed everything on me. I knew she was out to get me, so I ran.

Saturday: You were afraid even after God answered your prayer for fire? and after he answered your prayer to let it rain?

Elijah: I guess so.

Friday: Where did you run?

Elijah: First, I ran to the desert. I sat under a tree and asked God to let me die.

Sunday: What happened then?

Elijah: What do you think? God took care of me. He sent an angel to give me food.

Saturday: Hmm. A food angel. Very interesting.

Elijah: Then I walked for forty days, climbed Mount Sinai, and hid in a cave.

Friday: Were you alone in the cave?

Elijah: Not exactly. I heard the voice of God speak to me.

Friday: Aha! What did the voice say?

Elijah: God told me to leave the cave and stand on the mountainside. Then an incredible wind began to blow.

Saturday: Was God in the wind?

Elijah: No. But then came an earthquake.

Sunday: Was God in the earthquake?

Elijah: No. Then came a fire.

Friday: Was God in the fire?

Elijah: No. God was not in the wind, the earthquake, or the fire. Instead, he spoke to me in a gentle whisper.

Friday: The God of the universe spoke to you in a gentle whisper? Now that's a surprise. What did God say to you?

Elijah: God promised to give me three helpers. And he told me that thousands of people in Israel had not worshiped the fake god Baal.

Friday: What do you have to say about this message from God?

Elijah: God is awesome! He knew I needed friends who would help me teach my people and lead them in the right path. I was ready to give up, but now I know that with God's help, I can go on!

Group: *(Hums* Dragnet *theme.)*

If you use this skit as a discussion starter, read aloud 1 Kings 19:11-13, then ask the following questions:

● **How did God speak to Elijah?**

● **How does God speak to us?**

● **When we listen, what kinds of things does God tell us?**

2 KINGS

" 'Where is the Lord, the God of Elijah?' "

2 Kings 2:14b

2 KINGS
5:1-14

THEME:
We can trust the Lord.

SUMMARY:
In this OBJECT LESSON, kids discover that we can trust the Lord even when the situation seems impossible.

PREPARATION: You'll need index cards, small drinking cups with mouths narrower than the index cards, dishpans of water, and paper towels. If weather permits, plan to do this activity outside.

Form trios, and give each trio an index card, a cup, and a dishpan of water. Provide paper towels in case of spills.

Say: **We're going to try an experiment that might seem impossible. I want one of you in each trio to dip the cup in the water and fill it about half-full. Now place the card over the top of the cup, and hold it there with your pointer finger. Quickly turn the cup upside down over the dishpan. Slowly remove your finger and . . . look!**

Kids will see that the index card seems to be holding the water in the cup, even when the cup is upside down. If the trick doesn't work the first time, allow kids to try again. Let each person in each trio have a turn. Then gather kids in a circle and ask:

● What surprised you about this experiment?

Say: Today we're going to hear the story of a man whose life got turned upside down just like the cups in our experiment. And just as in our experiment, everything turned out all right.

Read aloud 2 Kings 5:1-14. Ask:

● Whose life got turned upside down? What happened?

● What good thing happened that seemed impossible?

● In this story, how was God like the index card?

● What do you think Naaman learned about God?

Say: We can trust God even when things seem impossible. Remember, when your life seems to turn upside down, you can always trust in God.

2 KINGS 5:1-15

THEME:

We can rejoice in God's goodness.

SUMMARY:

With this MUSIC IDEA, kids have a rappin' good time rejoicing with Naaman, whose skin disease was cured when he dipped seven times in the Jordan River.

PREPARATION: You'll need a Bible, aluminum pie pans, and a photocopy of the rap on page 94.

Say: Today we're going to hear the story of a great general and celebrate his victory. The victory we're going to celebrate didn't happen in battle. Listen very carefully, and see if you can figure out what kind of victory this general won.

Read aloud 2 Kings 5:1-15. Then ask:

● What was this general fighting?

● How did he win?

● Was this an easy victory for General Naaman? Why or why not?

● What did Naaman discover about the God of Israel?

Say: General Naaman won a victory over a terrible skin disease by obeying the prophet Elijah. Let's have some fun celebrating with Naaman.

Have kids form six groups. Give each group a section of the rap. Distribute aluminum pie pans evenly among the groups.

Say: Work out rhythm and movements for the part of the rap you have. You can use the pie pans for hats, rhythm instruments, or props. Give kids three minutes to plan their presentations. Then bring everyone together in a large circle, and have each group perform its section of the rap.

1 I'm dipping one, two, One, two, three. There's no difference that I can see.	4 Shout it! Seven, six, Five, four, three. Look, I've been healed of my leprosy!
2 I'm dipping two, three, Two, three, four. Still no change—I'll dip three times more.	5 Singin' four, three, Four, three, two. I believe in God now. *(Clap.)* Don't you?
3 I'm dipping five, six, Five, six, seven. Praise the great God who lives in heaven!	6 Singin' three, two, one. I'll serve God in heaven— He's the only one!

2 KINGS 21:19-24; 22:1, 8

THEME:
God wants us to follow his lead.

SUMMARY:
Use this active DEVOTION to help kids experience the need for a trustworthy leader.

PREPARATION: You'll need a Bible and blindfolds.

EXPERIENCE

Find out which child will have the next birthday, and designate that child as the Leader. Have everyone put on blindfolds. Then say: (Leader) **is going to lead you through some exercises.** (Leader) **can't say anything out loud but can lead you with his** (or her) **actions. Go!**

Allow several seconds of confusion, then ask:
● **What seems to be the problem here?**
● **What can we do to fix it?**
● **Should I let the Leader take off the blindfold? Why?**
● **Should I let everybody take off their blindfolds? Why?**

RESPONSE

Say: **You can all take off your blindfolds and sit in a circle. The problem we just had reminds me of what happened to a young king. Let's read about it from the Bible. There are two kings in this story—listen for the name of the younger one, and see if you can guess what his problem was.**

Read aloud 2 Kings 21:19-24; 22:1. Then ask:

● What was the young king's name?

● How old was he?

Say: **Josiah was only eight years old when he became king, and his father had been a wicked king who led the people away from God.**

● What kinds of problems do you think Josiah faced?

Say: **When Josiah was eighteen years old, he decided to repair the Temple. The workers in the Temple made a wonderful discovery. Listen.** Read aloud 2 Kings 22:8. **The Book of the Teachings had been lost for a long time. But now it was found.** Ask:

● How would the Book of the Teachings help Josiah?

● How would not having God's teachings be like being blindfolded?

CLOSING

Say: **God's teachings help us know what to do and how to live. Living without God's teachings is hard—like trying to do exercises without being able to see or hear your leader. Now let's sing a song and do a fun exercise without blindfolds that will help us remember how important God's Word is to us.**

Lead kids in "The Bunny Hop" using these words:

Read your Bible often.
Pray every day.
That's how to live God's way.
HEY! HEY! HEY!

1 CHRONICLES

*" 'Sing to the Lòrd, all the earth. Every day
tell how he saves us.' "*

1 Chronicles 16:23

1 CHRONICLES 11:1-3

THEME:
God helps us grow up.

SUMMARY:
Use this AFFIRMATION ACTIVITY to help children affirm one another and feel confident about growing up.

PREPARATION: You'll need old magazines, white paper, scissors, glue sticks, and a pencil for each child. You'll also need a Bible. This activity works best for older kids who read and write.

Set out magazines. Give each child a sheet of white paper, and have children look through the magazines for pictures of what they might look like when they grow up. Have each child cut out one picture and glue it on the white paper.

Invite children to sit in a circle, and give each child a pencil. Have children write their names on the back of the papers. Say: **Please pass your picture to the person on your left. When everyone is holding a picture, look at the name on the back and write something nice about that person under his or her name. For example, "She is very kind" or "He is always polite."** Remind children that only good things are to be written on the papers.

Continue passing the papers to

the left until each child has written on all the papers. Then one at a time, have children stand and read aloud the affirmations they've received. As each child finishes, have the class clap and say: **You're special now, and you'll be special when you grow up!**

After all the children have shared, say: **In 1 Chronicles 11:1-3, God's chosen people needed to choose a king. They decided to ask David to be the king. They chose him because they remembered how brave and wise he had been as a child and later as a leader.** Read the passage aloud for the children.

Before children leave, tell them individually one way you see them growing in the Lord.

1 CHRONICLES
14:8-12

THEME:
Prayer is the best way to start everything.

SUMMARY:
Use this field TRIP to help children understand the importance of prayer.

PREPARATION: Choose a destination such as a local park or forest, and provide appropriate transportation. You'll need several index cards. On each card write one thing your kids need to do in preparation for their trip. For example, "Put on our name tags," "Choose a buddy to stay with at the park," "Line up to

go," and "Get in the cars." One card should say "Pray." On a table, lay the cards randomly with the words facing up.

As children arrive, direct them to look at the index cards. Say: **These are things we need to do before we go on our field trip today. Let's put the cards in order. We need to decide what to do first, second, and so on.** Give kids a few minutes to work together to put the cards in order. Then ask:

● **What helped you decide where to put the "pray" card?**

Say: **In 1 Chronicles 14:8-12, King David found out that the Philistines were going to attack his country. He had to decide what to do.** Ask:

● **What kinds of things do you think he needed to do to prepare for the upcoming attack?**

Give children time to answer, and then say: **King David had many things to do, but let's see what he did first.** Have a child volunteer to read aloud 1 Chronicles 14:8-10. Ask:

● **What did King David do before he did anything else?**

If children placed the prayer card in a position other than first, say: **As we prepare for our trip today, let's do what wise King David did and put prayer first.** Have a child put the prayer card on top.

If children placed the prayer card first in the pile, say: **You're wise the way David was wise. You know how important it is to pray first.**

Use the pile of cards in the order the children chose. Ask a volunteer to pray, then proceed with the rest of the tasks.

On the way to the park, discuss why praying first is a good idea. Remind kids that any time is a good time for prayer. After you arrive at the park, pray: **God, we thank you for King David, who remembered to pray first. Help us remember that any time is a good time to pray. In Jesus' name, amen.**

1 CHRONICLES 16:31-34

THEME:
God enjoys our praise.

SUMMARY:
In this creative PRAYER, children listen to and act out a prayer of King David.

PREPARATION: You'll need a variety of items, such as poster board, construction paper, markers, scissors, old magazines, wooden blocks, pie pans, spoons, yarn, and seashells. Add other items as desired. You'll also need Bibles.

Have children sit in a circle. Say: **King David had many talents. He was a good shepherd. He could play the harp. He was a great soldier. David also wrote beautiful prayers to God. Today I'm going to read part of a prayer David wrote. As I read it, I want you to try and picture in your mind the things David describes in his prayer.** Read aloud 1 Chronicles 16:31-34, then ask:

● **What things did you picture?**

Then say: **I'll read the prayer again. This time try and *hear* the things David describes.** Read the verses again, and give children time to tell what they heard.

Have children form four groups. Provide supplies and Bibles. Assign one verse to each group. Say: **Let's make something to show how these verses make us feel. You may want to make a poster or picture, write a song. or make up sound effects to go with your verse. You'll have five minutes to work on your projects. Then we'll share our praise prayers.**

As children work, mention how happy it makes God when we pray. Affirm each group's effort to create the prayer.

Have groups present their praise projects. Encourage children to clap after each group gives its verse and presentation. When each group has shared, say: **King David was talented at writing prayers, and so are you. God is pleased when we praise him.**

1 CHRONICLES 23:1-6

THEME:
Cooperative effort is music to God's ears.

SUMMARY:
Through this MUSIC IDEA, children learn that cooperation benefits everyone.

PREPARATION: Choose a familiar song, such as "Jesus Loves Me" or "The B-I-B-L-E." Write each word of the chorus or first line of the song on a separate sheet of white paper. Have one sheet for each child. You'll also need a Bible.

As children arrive, sing the song you'll be using for this activity. Encourage kids to join in as they arrive.

Gather the children in a circle, and ask a volunteer to read aloud 1 Chronicles 23:1-6. Then say: **These verses tell about Solomon becoming king. His father, King David, was old and would soon die. He knew running the Temple was a big job. So David assigned all the Levites, who were in charge of the Temple, specific jobs to do. If the people did their jobs well for the new king, Solomon, things would run smoothly.** Have children stand side by side facing you. Say: **Today I want to pretend that I am King Solomon. The work in my kingdom is a song. So I want to assign this word to each of you.** Hold up the sheet with the first word of the song. Say it out loud for younger children. **Now, do you all know your part? Let's sing the song.**

Lead children in singing a one-word song. Ask:

● **What's wrong? Don't you like the song?**

Say: **It doesn't work if we all sing the same word. Each of you needs a different word to sing to make a song.** Give a different word to each child.

Help children put the words of the song into the right order. Give special assistance to younger children or pair them with partners who can read.

Say: **You've cooperated to make a song just like the way King Solomon's people cooperated to make a happy kingdom. Cooperation is good for everyone. Let's sing our song in celebration! It makes God happy when we cooperate.**

Show children how they can sing the song by singing their words when you point to them. Practice several times. Clap after each time, and remind kids that cooperation means using their words and actions to help others.

2 CHRONICLES

" 'Now give me wisdom and knowledge so I can lead these people in the right way.' "

2 Chronicles 1:10a

2 CHRONICLES 1:7-13

THEME:
Wisdom is a gift from God.

SUMMARY:
Use this LEARNING GAME to help children discover what made Solomon a wise king.

PREPARATION: You'll need a Bible and six index cards. On the front of each card, write one letter of the word "wisdom." On the back, describe situations such as "You're not supposed to wear your brother's clothes without asking first, but you want to borrow his blue sweater for school today, and he's already gone. What do you do?" or "You're visiting your grandmother. When no one else is in the room, you break a lamp. But no one saw you do it. What do you do?" or "Your mom told you never to run in the house. You ran through the family room, fell, and cut your lip. Your mom is comforting you and asks you what happened. What do you say?"

Have children sit in a circle. Then say: **In 2 Chronicles, God appears to King Solomon and tells him that he can ask for anything he wants. Wow! That sounds exciting. He could have anything he wanted. Are you wondering what Solomon asked for? We're going to play a game to find out. Before we do that, try and guess.** Ask:

● **What do you think Solomon asked God for?**

If a child answers correctly, say: **That's right—wisdom is what King Solomon asked God for. Let's try out some wisdom with the situations written on the index cards.**

Shuffle the index cards, and then read the situations to the children. Discuss several options after each one. As kids answer each question, turn the card over and place it on the floor in order, spelling "wisdom."

After discussing all six of the situations, point out the word "wisdom" and say: **King Solomon could have asked God for anything in the world—money, power, a beautiful palace. But instead he asked for wisdom.** Read aloud 2 Chronicles 1:7-13. Say: **In our game you chose wise solutions to our problems. King Solomon was a good king because he was wise. Wisdom is a gift from God, and it's a good thing for all of us to ask for!**

2 CHRONICLES 5:1

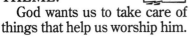

THEME:
God wants us to take care of things that help us worship him.

SUMMARY:
This active SERVICE PROJECT allows kids to help care for an item related to worship in your church.

PREPARATION: Secure permission for the children of your class to do a cleanup project on a special item related to worship in your church. Choose a job that requires some real effort. You'll need the cleaning items necessary for the task. You'll also need a Bible.

Read aloud 2 Chronicles 5:1. Say: **The Temple was full of valuable, special things to help people worship God.** Ask:

● **How many special things do you think our church has to help us worship God?**

Let children answer, then say: **Today we're going on a treasure hunt. Let's see how many of those special things we can find in our church.**

Take children on a tour of the church. Remind them that they need to be quiet since other classes are meeting. As you find "treasures," point them out to children. Go into the sanctuary to find candles, the altar, Bibles, hymnals, and any other items related to worship. Then show kids the item that needs special care. While they work, remind them how special the item is and how it helps people worship God.

Return to class and ask:

● **Which of the special items we saw today had you noticed before?**

● **How do you feel since you helped care for something that helps people worship God?**

● **How do you think King Solomon felt about the Temple?**

● **What can we do each day to remind ourselves of the importance of worshiping God?**

As kids leave, thank them for their part in helping others worship God.

2 CHRONICLES 7:1-3

THEME:
God is with us.

SUMMARY:
In this QUIET REFLECTION, children learn that God is always with us.

PREPARATION: You'll need construction paper, scissors, and tape. In your classroom, set up a small table to use as an altar. Cover the table with a cloth or sheet. Provide two candles in sturdy candleholders, matches, and a Bible. You'll also need a cassette of quiet praise music and a tape player.

Set out construction paper and scissors. As children enter, ask each one to make a symbol or picture of church or God. It might be a cross, Bible, heart, or rainbow. When they have each made a symbol, say: **When Solomon built the Temple for God, all the people came to celebrate. Now we're going to gather like the people did.**

Have children gather around the altar you've set up. As they do, have them tape their symbols on the cloth covering it. Tell kids their symbols make the altar extra-special. Then give two children each a candle in a holder and give another child the Bible. Tell children that you will tell them when to place their objects on the altar.

Begin playing the soft music, and dim the lights. Ask children to place the candles on the altar, then have the child place the Bible on the altar. Then have an older child carefully light the candles. Say: **I'm going to read the story of the people of God gathering for the first time in that Temple. As I read, I want you to pretend that you are there.**

Read aloud 2 Chronicles 7:1-3. Pause for a moment of silence. Ask:

● **What do you think it was like for the people who were there on the first day of worship in that Temple?**

● **How do you think they felt?**

● **What do you think it was like to know that God was actually there among them?**

Let children share. Say: **God was with the Israelites that day in a special way. God promises to always be with us, too. Sometimes we don't feel as if he's with us, but he is! This story helps us to remember that.**

Share a personal experience about a time when you've felt God especially close. Ask children to share times they've felt God's presence in a special way. Close in prayer, thanking God for always being with us.

2 CHRONICLES 9:22-28

THEME:
All blessings come from God.

SUMMARY:
This OBJECT LESSON helps children see how richly God blessed Solomon.

PREPARATION: You'll need a globe and a basket filled with "treasures," such as a crown, rings, jewelry, old perfume bottles, and imitation gold coins. You'll also need a "royal robe" and a chair for a "throne." An instant-print camera is optional but can add a lot of fun. Put the throne against one wall. Place the globe and basket of treasures in the middle of the room. You'll also need a Bible.

Gather children around the throne and say: **Let's pretend that this is King Solomon's throne. He was a good king who listened to God and tried to do what was right. The Bible tells us that God blessed Solomon.** Read aloud 2 Chronicles 9:22-28.

Choose one child to be King Solomon, and have him or her sit on the "throne." Tell the other children that as kings and queens from all over the world, they will take riches to Solomon the way the Bible tells us royalty did. Have children take turns spinning the globe and pointing randomly to a spot on it to choose a country to be from. After each child has pointed to a country, announce in a regal voice:

King Solomon, I present (child's name) **from** (the country pointed to). Have each child take a treasure to Solomon. After each child has had a turn, Solomon should look very wealthy!

Repeat the game until everyone has had a turn as King Solomon. Each time a new Solomon is chosen, read aloud 2 Chronicles 9:22. You may wish to take a picture of each child sitting on the throne surrounded by treasures. Allow the "kings and queens" to take their pictures home.

After everyone has been Solomon, ask:
● **How was receiving these treasures like receiving blessings from God? How was it different?**
● **Why did these people bring treasures to Solomon?**
● **How did Solomon get to be so wise?**
● **Why did God bless Solomon with such great wisdom?**

Say: **Solomon was blessed by God because he listened to God and did what was right. Let's try to always do what God wants us to do just as Solomon did in our lesson today.**

2 CHRONICLES
24:1-14

THEME:
God wants us to share with others.

SUMMARY:
Through this SERVICE PROJECT, children discover how love grows when we share it.

PREPARATION: You'll need a clay flower pot, ribbon, buttons, glue, a potted plant, a bag of soil, and a small jar of water. Add other items as desired or needed to allow each child to hold one item. You'll also need a Bible.

As children arrive, give each of them one of the items listed above and say: **I'm giving this to you. This is yours.**

After all the children have arrived and all the supplies have been given out, say: **In 2 Chronicles 24:1-14, a king named Joash noticed that the Temple had not been cared for. So he took a huge box and placed it in the center of town and asked everyone to put money in it for the rebuilding of the Temple.** Everyone gave money, and the Temple was repaired.

I've given each of you a gift as you came in today. Now I need your help. I know someone who lives alone and needs cheering up. If we work together, we could make a lovely gift for that person. But we all must give what we have.

Ask kids to share what they've been given the way the people in today's Bible passage did. Have them decorate the pot with ribbon and buttons and then place the plant and the soil in the pot. Have one child water it. Then display it next to you. Ask:

● **How do you think the people felt when they helped care for the Temple by giving their money?**

● **What was it like to work together to make a special gift?**

● **How do you think the person who gets this plant will feel?**

● **How do you think God feels when we do things like this?**

Say: **God is pleased when we share with others what God has given to us. Thanks for helping me today and for your willingness to share.**

If possible, have children accompany you to deliver the plant.

EZRA

" 'The Lord our God has been kind to us.' "

Ezra 9:8b

EZRA
7:10-16

THEME:
Church workers deserve our appreciation.

SUMMARY:
In this PARTY idea for workers in your church, children examine Ezra's call to ministry and see people in the church who are answering the same call.

PREPARATION: You'll need Bibles, newsprint, construction paper, markers, art supplies, party decorations, and a list of church staff. Check with the church secretary to set a date for the party. Plan this lesson for two sessions: session one to plan the party and session two to enjoy it!

Begin by helping children find the book of Ezra in the Bible. Then say: **Ezra was a man who loved God. The Bible tells us that Ezra tried to always do what God wanted him to do.** Read aloud Ezra 7:10. Say: **Ezra spent his whole life working in service to God. In our church we have people who work for God.** Ask:
● **Who are some of the workers in our church?**
Brainstorm and write the names and jobs on newsprint. Say: **Since these people all work so hard to serve God, why don't we give them a party to show how much we appreciate them?**
Have children give ideas for the

party. Decide on food, games to play, decorations, and awards for each person.

Form four groups. Have Group 1 write invitations to the people listed on the newsprint. Make sure some of the children in this group are able to write. Ask younger children to decorate the invitations and to help seal the envelopes. Have an adult helper deliver the invitations. Group 2 can plan decorations, while Group 3 makes award certificates. Allow Group 4 to plan games and activities for the party. Ask parents to help provide the food and drinks.

When you hold the party, tell the guests that you're studying about Ezra, a man who felt called to work for God. Have each guest share why they decided to work in the church. Then play games, give awards, and enjoy! This will be a gift to the church workers that they will never forget and an encouragement to the children as well!

EZRA
10:1-3

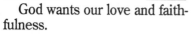

THEME:
God wants our love and faithfulness.

SUMMARY:
This active DEVOTION helps each child experience a close covenant with a friend.

PREPARATION: Prepare one strong one-by-twelve-inch felt strip for each pair of children. Place puzzles, books, games, and blocks in different areas around the room. You'll also need a Bible and scissors.

EXPERIENCE
As children enter, let them choose activities they'd like to do. Ask them to wait for instructions before beginning the activities.

After all the children have arrived, say: **We're going to hear a Bible story about a man named Ezra. Ezra got very upset because of all the bad things God's people were doing. In fact, he got so upset that he lay down in front of the Temple and cried. The people responded and told Ezra they would stop being bad and would do what God wanted. In Ezra 10:3 the people said, " 'Now let us make an agreement before our God.' " They decided to make a covenant with God.** Ask:

● **What do you think a covenant is?**

Say: **I'm going to help you understand what a covenant is.**

Have children form pairs and stand side by side. Using the felt strips, tie each pair together by joining their inside wrists. Ask them to raise their joined hands in a pledge. Lead them in saying to each other, "I promise and covenant to stay with you."

Encourage pairs to begin the activities with their wrists tied together. Let them have a few minutes to experience their "covenant relationships."

RESPONSE
After five to seven minutes, gather children together. Ask:

● **How did it feel to be paired**

with another person?

● How is being tied together like having a covenant with someone?

Give kids time to share and then untie them.

Say: **The people in the story made a promise or covenant with God to stay close to him and only do the things he wanted them to do.** Ask:

● **How do you think the people felt about making this covenant?**

● **What kind of covenants with God do people make today?**

● **Do you have any covenants with God? Explain.**

CLOSING

Cut each strip of felt in half lengthwise, and give one piece to each child. Say: **God has made a covenant with us to always love and watch over us. Take this felt strip home, and put it where you'll see it every day as a reminder of God's covenant with you.**

NEHEMIAH

"I prayed to the God of heaven."

Nehemiah 1:4b

NEHEMIAH 2:2-8

THEME:
God answers prayer.

SUMMARY:
In this SKIT, patterned after the game show *I've Got a Secret,* guest panelists try to guess why the king granted Nehemiah's request.

NEHEMIAH'S SECRET

SCENE: A game show stage with a video-action scene of Nehemiah visiting the king with a request.

PROPS: You'll need an "Applause" sign, a videotape, and a cup fit for a king.

CHARACTERS:
Host
Hostess
Panelist 1: Jimbo
Panelist 2: Claudine
Panelist 3: Seymour
Contestant: Nehemiah
King Artaxerxes (ar-tah-ZERK-sees)
Audience

SCRIPT

Host: Welcome to the game show of the hour *It's My Secret!*

Hostess: *(Holds up Applause sign. Audience cheers.)*

Host: I'd like to introduce you to our three panelists. Our first panelist is Jimbo Blob. Tell us about yourself, Jimbo.

Jimbo: *(Talking like a country boy)* Well, me and the missus farm chickens in Kansas.

Hostess: *(Holds up Applause sign. Audience cheers.)*

Host: *(Turns to Panelist 2.)* Now let's hear from Claudine Cowlick.

Claudine: Aren't you sweet! I'm from New Mexico, and my hobbies are hang gliding and bake-offs!

Hostess: *(Holds up Applause sign. Audience cheers.)*

Host: Well, that brings us to Seymour Sanders. You're from New York, aren't you?

Seymour: *(Talking tough)* Yeah, you want to make something of it?

Host: *(Laughing nervously)* Uh no, but I would like to introduce the three of you to today's contestant. Come on out, Nehemiah! *(Nehemiah enters stage.)*

Hostess: *(Holds up Applause sign. Audience cheers.)*

Host: Nehemiah has a secret. Let's have him tell you his story.

Nehemiah: My people were slaves to the king. I was his food tester. I made sure his food had no unpleasant additives.

Host: Tell us about your secret.

Nehemiah: *(Holds up videotape.)* Let me show you my video.

Host: *(Takes tape.)* That's a great idea, Nehemiah. We'll play it for our panelists. *(Host pretends to put tape into VCR.)*
(Nehemiah leaves his place and takes center stage with the King. Video action begins.)

Nehemiah: *(Sips from cup, and hands it to the King. Looks sad.)* Here you go, ol' King, it's poison free.

King: Thanks, Nehemiah. But why do you look so sad?

Nehemiah: I'm sad because my homeland lies in ruins.

King: Can I help?

Nehemiah: Send me home, so I can rebuild it.

King: All right! Stay as long as you need to, and take all the supplies you need. I'm writing letters to grant you safe passage though the land. *(Video action ends, and characters freeze in place.)*

Host: All right, panelists, who can guess Nehemiah's secret?

Seymour: *(Angrily)* How can we guess from that? Show it to us again. But faster!
(Host replays video, this time in fast-forward. Characters re-enact exact video sequence in FAST MOTION.)

Host: Panelists? What's Nehemiah's secret?

Claudine: I don't get it. Could you slow it down, please?
(Host replays video, this time in slow motion. Characters re-enact exact video sequence in SLOW MOTION.)

Host: Panelists? Got any ideas?

Jimbo: I don't know about you, but I'd say that old boy must have said a quiet prayer to the great Almighty before he got the pluck to ask that king for such a favor.

Host: You're right! Nehemiah gave God a major prayer for help. That's the secret!

Hostess: *(Holds Applause sign. Audience cheers.)*

If you use this skit as a discussion starter, here are possible questions:

- **What is prayer?**
- **Why should we pray?**
- **When can we talk to God?**
- **What happens when people pray?**

NEHEMIAH
4:1-23

THEME:
God wants us to stay focused on him.

SUMMARY:
Use this LEARNING GAME to show children the importance of staying focused on God even when distractions arise.

PREPARATION: You'll need a watch with a second hand and lots of blocks.

Say: Jerusalem was God's holy city. At one time it had a great wall around it to keep God's people safe. But Israel's enemies tore it down. Later Nehemiah and a band of Israelites began to rebuild it. In Nehemiah 4:1-23, it says that their enemies did everything they could to stop them from building the wall.

Have children form two groups. Have the first group be the Builders (Nehemiah and his friends). Its job is to build the wall for God. Have the second group be the Enemies. They are to do anything they can think of to stop the Builders but cannot touch the Builders or the wall.

Give Builders the blocks, and allow them three minutes to build the wall. Encourage the Enemies to be creative in distracting the Builders. You might suggest the Enemies look out the window and shout, "Wow, look at that!"; do a silly comedy routine to get the Builders to laugh; or pretend to get a drink and invite the Builders to come along.

After three minutes ask the Builders to stop working. Ask:

- **How did it feel to try and work while being distracted?**
- **How was this activity like Nehemiah's rebuilding of the city wall? How was it different?**
- **What made you able to keep working?**

Have kids switch roles, and let the second group be the Builders.

Then gather the children, and read aloud or summarize Nehemiah 4:1-23. Say: **Israel's enemies made fun of Nehemiah and his friends, tried to pick fights, and even threatened to kill them. They had a lot more distractions than you did.** Ask:

- **Why do you think they kept working?**
- **When you try to do something for God, what things tend to distract you?**
- **What are ways you can stay focused on God?**

Ask kids for help in putting the blocks away. As they pick up the blocks, have them pray silently, asking God to help them stay focused on him in the same way Nehemiah and his friends did.

NEHEMIAH
8:1-9

THEME:
God wants us to share his Word with others.

SUMMARY:
In this activity, children prepare a QUIET REFLECTION to share with church members.

PREPARATION: You'll need Bibles, poster board, markers, construction paper, scissors, and glue. You'll also need to make arrangements for the children to read Scriptures during your church's worship service.

Hold up a Bible and ask:
● **What stories do you know from the Bible?**
Allow children time to answer. Then say: **You know lots of stories from the Bible. Did you know that a long time ago, God's people had not read the Bible for so long that they forgot all the stories in it? They asked Nehemiah to read it to them.** Read aloud Nehemiah 8:1-4a, 5-9.

Explain to children that they are going to read God's Word to God's people the way Nehemiah did. Select two or more children to read passages of Scripture. Let kids choose the verses they want to read, and give them a few minutes to practice. Have the other children make posters to remind the congregation that God's Word is sacred and important.

As children work, discuss how Nehemiah felt as he got ready to face the Israelites. Ask:
● **How do you think Nehemiah felt as he faced the Israelites?**
● **How do you feel?**
● **Why is it important to share God's Word and listen to it?**
Have kids carry in their posters and share their Scripture passages at the appropriate time in the worship service.

NEHEMIAH
10:32-39

THEME:
God wants us to give generously.

SUMMARY:
This active DEVOTION helps children better understand the concept of tithing.

PREPARATION: You'll need an envelope for each child with one of the following job titles written on the front: "priest," "Levite," "gatekeeper," "singer," or "servant." Make construction paper coins, and place either ten, twenty, or thirty coins inside each envelope. Each coin is equal to "one dollar." You'll also need a Bible.

EXPERIENCE
As children arrive, give them each an envelope. Help kids read their job titles on the envelopes. Announce that you are Nehemiah and say: **Money is needed to pay**

the Temple workers and to buy important things for God's house. Ask:

● How can we gather enough money to take care of God's house? Do you have any ideas?

Say: I suggest we all pitch in. Encourage children to open their envelopes and count their coins. Say: If all of you gave ten coins, that would leave some with no money left to buy food for their families. Others would have a lot left.

Then suggest that they all give a tithe. Say: A tithe is one-tenth of whatever you have. If you have ten dollars, one-tenth is a dollar. Encourage those with ten dollars to give one coin. For those who have twenty dollars, one-tenth is two dollars. Encourage those kids to give two coins. For those with thirty dollars, a tithe is three dollars. Have them contribute three coins.

RESPONSE

Count the money you have collected, and ask children to count their money. Say: Nehemiah and the people all gave part of what they had. They gave with joy and happiness. Read aloud Nehemiah 10:37-39. Ask:

● How did it feel to give some of your coins?

● Was it easier to give one coin or three coins?

● Why do you think God wants us to give back part of what he's given us?

● How do you think people's giving today compares to the way Nehemiah's people gave?

● What could you give to the church besides money?

CLOSING

Say: Take home one of your coins, and put it on your mirror or dresser so that you'll see it every day. When you see it, think of what you can give to the Lord. You can give your time, money, kindness, and love to God. I hope you will give as gladly as the people in our story.

NEHEMIAH
12:27-43

THEME:
God wants us to praise him with joy.

SUMMARY:
In this MUSIC IDEA, kids praise God and celebrate.

PREPARATION: You'll need rhythm instruments and two poster boards. Write the text of Nehemiah 12:27 on one poster board and Nehemiah 12:43 on the other. Plan to have this activity in a large outdoor area.

TEACHER TIP
If you are unable to enjoy this activity in a large open field, you could use a gymnasium. Plan to rejoice with joyful sounds!

Have children form two groups. Have Group 1 choose a favorite praise song, select instruments, and go out into the field. Then have

Group 2 choose a praise song, get its instruments, and face the first group.

With groups facing each other, say: **Our lesson today is about a very happy day for Nehemiah and the people of God. They finished building a huge wall around God's holy city, Jerusalem. And they were very happy.**

Have Group 1 read aloud the first poster board in unison. Then have Group 2 read the second.

Say: **We're going to have a celebration. Let's show each other how well we can celebrate. Group 1, let's hear you celebrate!** Encourage Group 1 to sing its song and play its instruments. Have Group 2 applaud and congratulate them on their performance. Then give Group 2 a turn to celebrate. Have Group 1 clap and cheer for them, too.

Say: **In Nehemiah's celebration the people could be heard all over the land. So let's celebrate again. This time let's stand further apart.** Repeat the celebration with groups standing further apart on the field. Repeat again, if time permits. Encourage groups to celebrate loudly so they can be "heard far away."

Say: **It's wonderful to see you having fun and laughing while you praise God and celebrate! Nehemiah and the people had a great time when they praised God too!**

ESTHER

" 'Then I will go to the king, even though it is against the law, and if I die, I die.' "

Esther 4:16b

ESTHER
2:5-11

THEME:
Families are important.

SUMMARY:
Use this QUIET REFLECTION activity to help children thank God for important people in their lives.

PREPARATION: You'll need a Bible, stationery, envelopes, and pencils or pens.

Begin by reading aloud Esther 2:5-11. Say: **Because Esther was the queen, she was able to save her people from being de-**

TEACHER TIP
This activity involves writing, so you'll want to pair younger children with older helpers or encourage the younger ones to draw pictures.

stroyed. But without Mordecai's help in raising her, Esther might not have been brave enough to stand up for her people. So Esther and Mordecai were a big help to each other. Today we're going to take some quiet time and think about the people we love and who love us.

Give each child two or three sheets of stationery and a pencil or pen. Ask kids to sit quietly and write a letter to someone who loves them. Give children a few minutes to complete their letters. As they're working, provide ideas for those needing help.

After they finish, have children sit in a circle and lay their letters in the center. Pray: **Heavenly Father, we've placed letters to people we love in the center of this circle. Please help those we love and watch over them. Thank you for all the people that we love and all those who love us. In Jesus' name, amen.**

Encourage children to personally deliver their letters.

ESTHER
4:6-16

THEME:
God wants us to do what we know is right.

SUMMARY:
In this SKIT, Brittany watches a TV show about Queen Esther and realizes how important it is to do the right thing. This activity requires reading and is best for third-graders and up.

QUEEN ESTHER MAKES A CHOICE

SCENE: Brittany sits to the side of the stage and addresses the audience as the center-stage action takes place.

PROPS: You'll need a Bible for discussion following the skit.

CHARACTERS:
Brittany
Mordecai
Hathach
Queen Esther

SCRIPT
Brittany: *(To audience)* My friend Joanne is feeling really down. Things have been pretty rough in her life lately. I want to tell her that God loves her, but if I tell her she might laugh at me. *(Sits on chair, dejected.)* Maybe I'll just stay home and watch TV. *(Pretends to turn on and watch TV. Mordecai and Hathach quickly take their places center stage and pantomime talking to each other. Brittany turns back to audience.)* Oh, a movie about Queen Esther is on. Her story is in the Bible. I think I'll watch!

Mordecai: *(Speaking aloud)* Hathach, will you give my niece Esther this note? It's a matter of life and death!

Hathach: The queen is your niece? I'll deliver the message at once. *(Mordecai and Hathach exit. Queen Esther enters and sits in a chair center stage. Hathach enters.)*

Hathach: Greetings, Your Highness! Your uncle gave me this note to give you!

Esther: Thank you, Hathach. *(Opens it, and reads silently. Suddenly looks afraid and drops the note.)*

Hathach: My queen! Is it bad news?

Esther: The worst. Uncle Mord says Haman has talked the king into killing my people! He says it's up to me to ask the king to stop Haman!

Hathach: *(Looks afraid.)* But if you go to see the king without an invitation, he might not point his scepter toward you—and you know what that means!

Esther: I would be killed! Tell Uncle Mord I cannot go! *(Begins to pace.)*
(Hathach is joined by Mordecai on stage. They pantomime a serious discussion. Mordecai exits.)

Hathach: *(To Esther)* Your uncle says if you refuse to help, God will use another. But he believes God may have allowed you to be the queen for just such a time as this!

Esther: *(After thinking a few seconds)* He's right. Tell Uncle Mordecai to have people pray for me. After three days of prayer, I will go to the king! If I die, I die. *(Both exit.)*

Brittany: *(Gets up, and pretends to turn off TV.)* Hmm. God made Esther queen so she could help her people. Maybe God made me Joanne's friend so I could tell her that God loves her. I think I'll go talk to Joanne right now. I might be embarrassed, but if she laughs, she laughs! *(Exits.)*

If you use this skit as a discussion starter, suggested Bible reading and questions follow.

Read aloud Esther 4:6-16. Ask:

● **Why was it important for Esther to try to save her people?**

● **What did Esther risk when she went to the king?**

● **Why do you think Brittany was afraid to tell Joanne that God loved her?**

● **Who might God want you to tell about him?**

● **What will you say to that person?**

JOB

" 'The Lord gave these things to me, and he has taken them away. Praise the name of the Lord.' "

Job 1:21b

JOB 1:13-22

THEME:
God rewards faithfulness.

SUMMARY:
This CRAFT helps children tell the story of how Job stayed true to God even in the midst of terrible disasters.

PREPARATION: You'll need paper plates, scissors, crayons or markers, a hole punch, and brass fasteners. You'll also need to make an example of the craft for children to see ahead of time. For younger children, write Job 1:22 on the plates before class. You'll also need a Bible.

Give each child a paper plate, and show kids how to fold it into four equal sections. After folding the plates, have children open up their plates and write in the center, "In all this Job did not sin or blame God" (Job 1:22).

In the top left section of the plate, have each child write the number "1" and draw oxen and donkeys. In the top right, have the children write the number "2" and draw camels and a servant. In the bottom left part of the plate, have kids write a number "3" and draw a house. And in the bottom right, have them write a number "4" and draw a picture of Job.

After the drawings are complete, have each child cut the plate apart on the folds and place all four sections on top of each other in numerical order. Then, using a hole punch, have each child make a hole one-quarter inch from the corner through all four sections of the plate and place a brass fastener through the hole.

Have children practice fanning open the plate one picture at a time so that the Scripture is revealed. Then tell them this story:

Job was a very good man, but sometimes bad things happen to good people. Many bad things happened to Job. First, evil men came and stole his oxen and donkeys and killed his servants. *(Have children show Section 1.)*

Then his camels were stolen and the servants caring for them were killed. *(Have children open their plates to Section 2.)*

Next Job's house fell down and his seven children were killed. *(Have children open their plates to Section 3.)*

After all of that happened, Job got sick and almost died. *(Have children open their plates to Section 4.)*

All of these bad things happened to Job. But the Bible tells us: *(have children read the Scripture on their plates)* **"In all this Job did not sin or blame God."**

Let children take turns telling the story of Job. Ask:

● **What bad things happen to us?**

● **How can we be like Job in our lives?**

Have kids take their plates home to tell their parents the story of Job.

PSALMS

"The Lord is my shepherd."

Psalm 23:1a

PSALM 1

THEME:
God helps us when we walk with him.

SUMMARY:
Use this PARTY idea to help kids see the benefits of walking with God.

PREPARATION: You'll need supplies as described below for the activities you choose.

As an icebreaker, have kids work together to build a strong tree that produces yummy fruit. Roll and twist brown paper or grocery bags to form a tree trunk and branches. Use brown packaging tape to secure the tree to a wall. Have kids add torn-paper leaves and then tape on sticks of Juicy Fruit gum for "fruit."

Gather kids in a circle "under" the tree. Distribute Bibles, and have a volunteer read aloud Psalm 1. Then form six groups, and secretly give each group one of the six verses of Psalm 1. Give groups two minutes to plan, then have them act out their verses. Let the groups who are observing guess which verse is being acted out.

After all the groups have performed, ask:

● **What advice does this psalm give us?**

● **What promises do you find in this psalm?**

● **What happens to a tree that**

grows by a river?

● **How is a good person like that?**

Play simple games using fruit that comes from strong, healthy trees. Let children bob for apples, juggle oranges between partners, and balance bananas on their noses. Encourage kids to handle the oranges and bananas gently because they'll be peeled later for treats.

To prepare treats, have kids wash their hands, and form three groups: the Peelers, the Choppers, and the Scoopers. After the Peelers have peeled the fruit, have the Choppers cut it into chunks for a fruit salad. The Scoopers can scoop individual servings into paper cups. Set out maraschino cherries, minimarshmallows, and whipped topping. Let kids sprinkle cherries and marshmallows into their fruit cups, then add dollops of whipped topping.

Close the party with prayer, asking God to help each child grow strong in the Lord. As kids leave, encourage them to "pick" the Juicy Fruit gum from the tree they made earlier.

PSALM
8

THEME:
We are important to God.

SUMMARY:
Use this AFFIRMATION ACTIVITY to help children understand their importance to God.

PREPARATION: You'll need a Bible, a garland of foil stars, glitter glue, scraps of construction paper, skinny Mylar streamers, gold metallic thread, and tape.

Before class, shape the star garland into a spiral with an eight- or nine-inch radius. Cut bright-colored construction paper into four-inch circles. Use a hole punch to make a hole one-half inch from the edge of each circle.

Ask:
● **When you look at the world around you, what reminds you of God's greatness?**

Say: **Looking at the night sky with all its brilliant stars reminded David of God's greatness. Let's read what he wrote.**

Read aloud Psalm 8:1-3. Then say: **Looking at the stars also made David wonder about something. Listen carefully to see if you can discover what David wondered about.** Read aloud verses 5-8, then ask:

● **What did David wonder about?**

● **Why do you think people are so important to God?**

● **How has God shown you that you are important to him?**

Set out the star garland you've shaped into a spiral, the construction paper circles, the glitter glue, the tape, and the streamers. Say: **This spiral of stars will represent God's beautiful heavens. Choose a construction paper circle and five streamers. Thread and tie the streamers through the hole in your circle. Then hold your circle so the streamers are at the bottom, and use glitter glue to**

write your name in the center of your circle.

As kids are working, distribute one-foot lengths of gold metallic thread. Have each child tape one end of the thread to the top of his or her circle. When kids have finished, call one child to bring his or her circle and attach the other end of the thread to the star garland. As the child ties the circle to the spiral, have the rest of the kids join you in saying: (Child's name) **is important to God. Hooray for** (child's name)! Continue until all the kids have attached their circles and been affirmed. Then hold up the sparkling spiral and ask:

● **What does this sparkling spiral remind you of?**

Say: **We'll hang this in our classroom as a reminder that our great and wonderful God values each of us very much!**

PSALM 23

THEME:
The Lord is my shepherd.

SUMMARY:
In this active DEVOTION, kids learn why it's important to have a loving shepherd they can trust.

PREPARATION: Gather a Bible, saltine crackers, peanut butter, napkins, blindfolds, a pitcher of lemonade, and cups. Place the lemonade and the cups in a darkened room a little distance from the room where you usually meet. Spread a thick coat of peanut butter on the crackers. You'll need to prepare two crackers for each student.

EXPERIENCE

Set out a napkin and two peanut butter crackers for each student. Say: **Welcome to the peanut butter cracker challenge! I'd like to see if you can eat both your crackers in one minute or less. Be careful not to eat so fast that you choke. Ready? Go!**

Applaud kids' efforts, then ask:

● **How would a nice cold drink of lemonade sound right now?**

Say: **The lemonade I have for you is in a different location. I'm going to lead you there. But first, everyone needs to put on a blindfold.**

Help kids put on blindfolds, then say: **Everyone huddle close to me, and I'll lead you to lemonade!** Lead kids to the darkened room and say: **The lemonade is somewhere in this room. I hope you can find it. You'll need to keep your blindfolds on. Please search carefully and slowly so you don't bump into furniture or a wall or each other.**

Let kids search the room blindfolded for a couple of minutes or until someone finds the pitcher of lemonade.

RESPONSE

Have kids take off their blindfolds, turn on the lights, and pour a cup of lemonade for everyone. As kids enjoy the lemonade, read aloud Psalm 23. Then ask:

● **In this activity, how were you like sheep?**

● **How was I like a shepherd?**
● **How could I have been a better shepherd?**

CLOSING

Say: **As a young boy, David watched his father's sheep. He knew that sheep are helpless. They have no way to defend themselves from attack by wolves or mountain lions. Many animals can smell water, but sheep can't—they have to be led to water or they'll die of thirst.** Ask:

● **If you were a sheep, what would you want your shepherd to be like?**
● **How is God like that?**

Close with prayer, thanking God for being a faithful shepherd.

PSALM
33:13-22

THEME:
God knows our hearts.

SUMMARY:
This LEARNING GAME helps children understand that God watches and understands us.

PREPARATION: You'll need a Bible and an old sheet to use as a screen. Cut two "peek" holes in the center of the sheet.

Set a table on its side to form a screen. Form two groups. Have Group 1 join you in hiding behind the table. Have Group 2 face the opposite wall so they can't see what Group 1 is doing. Choose two people from Group 1 to hold up the sheet by its top two corners. Encourage the holders to remain hidden behind the sheet.

Silently choose a child to step up to the sheet and peek through the eyeholes. Then have Group 2 turn around but remain at least five feet away from the table. Give Group 2 three chances to guess whose eyes are peeking through the holes in the sheet. Then let the other members of Group 1 take turns peeking through the sheet. After everyone's had a turn, have Group 1 and Group 2 switch places and repeat the peeking and guessing game.

Gather everyone in a circle and ask:

● **How could you tell who was peeking through the sheet?**
● **How did it feel to be the peeker?**
● **What's it like when you know someone is watching you?**

Say: **Someone** *is* **watching you!** Read aloud Psalm 33:13-22, then ask:

● **Who is watching you?**
● **Who else is God watching?**
● **What kinds of things does God see that we can't see?**
● **How does knowing that God is watching us give you hope?**

PSALM
51:1-13

THEME:
God gives us clean hearts when we confess our sins.

SUMMARY:
This QUIET REFLECTION helps children "see" how completely God forgives us.

PREPARATION: You'll need a Bible, a large mirror, a jar of petroleum jelly, paper towels, and a spray bottle of glass cleaner.

Say: **Although King David loved and followed God, he sometimes did wrong things and sinned against the God he loved. But David knew that God would forgive him. Let's read what David wrote when he needed to ask God for forgiveness.** Have volunteers read aloud Psalm 51:1-13. Ask:

● **How was David feeling when he wrote this psalm?**

● **What would you say to God if you sinned?**

Say: **Even though God knows all about the bad things we've thought and said and done, God loves us so much that he's always willing to forgive us. Let's do something interesting to see what God's forgiveness is like.**

Lead kids to the large mirror. Pass around the jar of petroleum jelly and say: **Take a little blob of petroleum jelly and rub it on the mirror as you think about a time you did something wrong.**

Model what you'd like kids to do by quietly rubbing a blob of petroleum jelly on the mirror. Then say: **Please be quiet and thoughtful as you do this.**

When kids finish, say: **Please bow your heads, and pray with me.** Pray a prayer similar to this one: **Dear God, we praise you because you are a holy and loving God. We're sorry for the wrong things we've done. Please forgive us for those things and make us clean again. Help us know the joy your forgiveness brings. In Jesus' name, amen.**

Distribute the paper towels and the spray cleaner. Let children take turns spraying and wiping the mirror until it's completely clean. Point out that when God forgives us, he makes our hearts as beautiful and clean as the shiny mirror.

PSALM
61:1-4

THEME:
God protects us.

SUMMARY:
Use this active DEVOTION to help children experience the security of God's protection.

PREPARATION: You'll need chairs, tables, blankets and sheets. You may also want to provide clothespins, duct tape, and rope. You'll need a Bible for the Closing.

EXPERIENCE
Encourage children to build a

"strong tower" or "fortress" from the materials you've provided. Have them make their fortress large enough for everyone to fit inside.

RESPONSE

When the fortress is complete, crawl inside with the kids and ask:
● **Why do people build fortresses?**
● **Do you think a fortress could protect people today? Why or why not?**
● **When do you feel especially safe and protected?**

CLOSING

Read aloud Psalm 61:1-4, then ask:
● **Who was David's fortress?**
● **Can God be our fortress today? Explain.**
● **When do you need God's protection?**
Say: **We're going to leave our fortress now, but we can always count on God's protection.**

As kids leave the fortress, have them say, "God is my protection."

PSALM 67

THEME:
All the people of the world can praise God.

SUMMARY:
Use this SERVICE PROJECT to help children spread the good news of God's love.

PREPARATION: You'll need a Bible, a map of the world, large sugar cookies, chocolate frosting, green-tinted vanilla frosting, blue-tinted vanilla frosting, chocolate chips, plastic knives, and a tray.

Say: **God's love is good news for people everywhere! Today we're going to celebrate God's love by making creation cookies. Before we begin, listen carefully as I read Psalm 67. See if you can discover who should praise God.** Read aloud Psalm 67, then ask:
● **Who should praise God?**
● **Why should all the people of the earth praise God?**
● **What can we praise God for?**

Display the map of the world. Then set out sugar cookies, frosting, chocolate chips, and plastic knives. Give each child two cookies to decorate to look like our world. Encourage kids to use the different colors of frosting to make the land and sea and to add chocolate chips for mountain ranges.

Help kids arrange the decorated cookies on a large tray. Say: **Let's carry our creation cookies to another class. Then we can share them and praise God together.**

Visit a class of senior citizens or another class of your choice. Have the children explain what the cookies stand for and why it's important to praise God. Have each person in the room praise God for one thing, then let children serve the cookies.

PSALM
90:14-17

THEME:
God gives us hope for the future.

SUMMARY:
Use this creative PRAYER to help children place their hopes for the future in God's hands.

PREPARATION: You'll need a Bible; markers; an empty, round oatmeal box; newsprint; packing tape; an instant-print camera; and strips of red, white, and blue paper.

Say: **It's exciting to think about the future.** Ask:
● **What do you think will be different about our world in twenty-five years? in fifty years?**
Say: **It's hard to imagine what our world will be like fifty or a hundred years from now. But we do know that God is in charge of our world and always will be. And since God loves us, we can hope and dream about wonderful things in our future. Let's see what Psalm 90:14-17 says about the future.**
Read aloud Psalm 90:14-17. Then ask:
● **What does the writer of this psalm ask God for?**
● **Do you think we can ask God for those same things? Why or why not?**
Say: **Let's put our prayers for the future in the form of a time capsule.** Pass out the markers and paper strips. **On the red strip,**

write or draw one hope you have for your future. Pause for kids to do this. **On the white strip, write or draw one thing you hope for the future of your family.** Pause. **On the blue strip, write or draw one thing you hope for the future of the whole world.**
Have kids drop their "hopes" into the oatmeal box. Then say: **To finish our time capsule, let's all write our names and ages on this sheet of newsprint, then wrap the box with it.**
Have kids decide when the time capsule should be opened—ten, twenty, or twenty-five years into the future. Mark that date on the newsprint after kids have signed it. Take an instant-print photograph of the whole group, of individual kids, or both. If you take individual photos, have kids sign the back of them. Then drop the photos into the box, wrap the box with the signed newsprint, and seal it with packing tape.
Gather kids in a circle, and place the time capsule in the center. Pray a prayer similar to this one: **Dear Lord, we don't know what will happen in the future, but you do. Thank you that we can trust you to take good care of us right now and in the future, too. Please bless each person here and help us do well as we try to live in a way that's pleasing to you. In Jesus' name, amen.**
Find an appropriate place in your church to store the time capsule.

PSALM 95:1-7a

THEME:
God enjoys it when we worship him through music.

SUMMARY:
Use this MUSIC IDEA to get kids excited about worshiping God.

PREPARATION: You'll need a Bible, a cassette or CD player, and cassettes or CDs of children's praise music.

Get a sing-along started with a simple version of *Name That Tune.* Have kids form groups of three to five. Play a few notes of a praise song, then stop the music. The first group to pop up and name the song can lead the rest of the kids in singing it. Make the game easier or harder by the number of notes you play before you stop the music. Repeat with four or five other songs. Then ask:

● **What's your favorite praise song? Why is it your favorite?**
● **How does singing praises to God make you feel?**
Read aloud Psalm 95:1-7a, then ask:
● **How do you think God feels when we sing praises?**
● **What are other places besides church where you enjoy singing praises to God?**
● **Why is it important to praise God in places other than church?**
Say: **Singing praises reminds us of how great God is, how** much God loves us, and how much God wants us to love him. It reminds us that we belong to the great and awesome God who created the whole world.

Close by leading kids in this cheer.
Clap your hands!
Stomp your feet!
We love you, God!
You're really neat!

PSALM 97:1-9

THEME:
Only God deserves our worship and praise.

SUMMARY:
With this CRAFT idea, children see that our God reigns supreme.

PREPARATION: You'll need a Bible, self-hardening clay, wax paper, and toothpicks.

Give each student a sheet of wax paper, a lump of self-hardening clay, and a toothpick. Encourage kids to model their favorite animals. Explain that they can mold the shapes with their hands and add details with the toothpicks. As kids finish, have them mark their initials on the bottom of their sculptures, then wash their hands.
Say: **Let's form a circle. Place your animal on the wax paper in front of you, then turn to a partner and tell something about the animal you made.**

After kids have shared, ask:

● **Would you ever think of praying to your clay animal? Why or why not?**

Say: **Praying to a lump of clay may sound silly to you, but in Bible times, many people worshiped statues made of wood or clay or carved from stone.** Ask:

● **How do you think God felt when he saw people worshiping statues and idols?**

Say: **Let's hear what Psalm 97 says about why we worship God and why it's silly to worship fake gods that are man-made.**

Have a volunteer read aloud Psalm 97:1-9. Then ask:

● **What reasons did you hear for worshiping God?**

● **What would you say to someone who worshiped a fake, man-made god?**

Close by having kids sing a praise song, such as "Our God Reigns" or "Awesome God."

PSALM 104

THEME:
We can praise God for his awesome creation.

SUMMARY:
During this field TRIP, children quietly enjoy God's handiwork.

PREPARATION: You'll need a Bible and paper lunch sacks. Each adult leader will need a watch.

Take a trip to a forest preserve or quiet park. Form groups of five children with one adult per group. Give each adult a paper lunch sack. Gather everyone and say: **We're going to go on a ten-minute silent nature hike. From the time you leave this group until the time you return, no one should talk at all. Listen carefully to the sounds of nature. If you need to communicate with someone, use hand gestures. As you're walking with your group, collect samples of interesting nature items, such as leaves, rocks, pine cones, and twigs— but be careful not to pick any wildflowers or disturb the environment.**

Have the adult leaders synchronize their watches and agree to meet again in ten minutes. Then send the groups out.

When everyone has returned, ask:

● **What kinds of sounds did you hear?**

● **Did you hear anything you've never heard before? Explain.**

● **What kinds of wildflowers did you see? What color were they? Did they have a fragrance?**

● **What kinds of animals did you see?**

● **Did you see any animal "houses"? What were they like?**

Let kids display the nature items they collected. Then say: **Listen to how the writer of Psalm 104 praises God for the wonderful things he sees in creation. Close your eyes as I read. Listen both to the psalm and to the sounds** of nature around us. Read aloud Psalm 104, then ask:

● **What have you learned about God from this nature hike?**

● **Why is it important for us to appreciate God's creation?**

Close with sentence prayers. Have each child finish the statement, "God, I praise you for..." by naming something they've observed in nature.

PSALM 105:1-5

THEME:
God wants us to seek him with our whole heart.

SUMMARY:
This LEARNING GAME encourages children to make knowing and loving God their first priority.

PREPARATION: You'll need a Bible and a bag of individually-wrapped treats. Choose a treat that's a favorite of your kids. Before kids arrive, hide the treats around the room. You'll need one treat for every child.

Gather kids in a circle and say: **I have a surprise for you to-day—a truly delicious surprise. All the surprises are hidden somewhere in this room, and there's a surprise for everyone. In just a moment, I'm going to let you search for a surprise. When you find one, bring it** back to this circle and gobble it up. Only find and bring back one surprise. Ready? Go!

As children enjoy their treats, ask:

● **Why did you all hurry to find your surprises?**

● **Do you always hurry to do the things your teachers ask you to do? Explain.**

● **What kinds of things are so important to you that you want to do them more than anything else?**

Say: **Psalm 105 talks about what's more important than anything else we could possibly do. Listen carefully to find out what that is.**

Read aloud Psalm 105:1-5. Ask:

● **What does this psalm say is the most important thing we can do?**

● **How is seeking God like seeking for treats? How is it different?**

● **How can we seek God?**

Say: **Turn to a partner and tell three ways you'll seek God this week.**

PSALM 111

THEME:
God wants us to know him.

SUMMARY:
Use this creative PRAYER to help children express praise to God.

PREPARATION: You'll need a Bible, bubble solution, and a bubble wand.

Say: **Psalm 111 tells us a lot about what God is like. Listen carefully for words that describe God.** Have volunteers read aloud Psalm 111. Ask:

● **What did you learn about God?**

● **What is God like?**

Say: **Great! You were good listeners. Now let's form a circle and pray in a truly unique way.** Hold up the bubble solution and wand. **I'll say, "Who is God?" I'll answer my own question with words from Psalm 111, such as "God does great things." Then I'll blow a stream of bubbles. When you catch or pop one of the bubbles, you'll repeat, "God does great things."**

Say: **Who is God? God does great things!"** Blow a stream of bubbles, and have kids repeat, "God does great things" as they catch or pop the bubbles. Then pass the bubbles to a child. Have him or her ask, "Who is God?" and answer with another statement and then blow a stream of bubbles. Repeat until everyone has had a turn.

PSALM 119:9-16

THEME:
God's Word is a great treasure.

SUMMARY:
Use this MUSIC IDEA to help children focus on the importance of God's Word.

PREPARATION: You'll need a Bible, paper, pencils, a cassette recorder, and a blank cassette.

Read aloud Psalm 119:9-16. Ask:

● **Why did the psalm writer feel that God's Word is important?**

● **What did the psalm writer do with God's Word?**

● **What can we do to show that we value God's Word?**

Say: **Psalm 119 says that paying attention to God's Word helps us live in a way that's pleasing to God. Most of the psalms were written as words to songs. I have a song we can sing about what we learned from this psalm. We'll sing it to the tune of "God Is So Good."**

God's Word is true.
God's laws are right.
And I'll obey them
With all my might.

Sing the chorus twice, then form groups of four, and give each group paper and a pencil. Say: **Now it's your turn to write a psalm. Choose a simple tune like "Row, Row, Row Your Boat," "Jesus Loves Me," or "Frère Jacques." Write your thoughts about God's Word to one of those tunes. It's OK if your psalm doesn't rhyme. I'll give you about five minutes to write your psalm.**

As kids work, circulate, offering help and encouragement. Give kids a one-minute warning, then call time. Have each group sing the psalm they wrote. If your kids aren't shy about being recorded, let them record their songs on a cassette.

PSALM 127

THEME:
Families are important to God.

SUMMARY:
Use this LEARNING GAME to reinforce the truth that God values families.

PREPARATION: You'll need a Bible, dress-up clothes, and four paper grocery bags. Place dress-up clothes suitable for a young child in one bag, for a teenager in another bag, for a mother in a third bag, and for a father in a fourth bag. Make sure you have the same number of dress-up items in each bag.

Say: **Today we're going to have fun learning about how families are important to God.**

Set the four bags of clothing at one end of the room. Have kids count off by fours to form teams. Have each team stand across the room from one of the bags.

Say: **This is a relay. You'll run to the bag, put on all the clothing items you find inside the bag, take the clothing off, and return it to the bag. Then run back, and tag the next person on your team.**

Make sure everyone understands the instructions, then start the relay. Have everyone applaud as each team finishes. Then gather kids in a circle, and read aloud Psalm 127. Ask:

● **What's great about being a** member of a loving family?

● **What's something about your family that you especially like?**

● **What makes a happy family?**

Say: **Turn to a partner, and tell one thing you'll do this week to show that you love your family.**

Close with prayer, asking God's blessing on the families of all the children.

PSALM 139:1-16

THEME:
God made us wonderfully.

SUMMARY:
In this AFFIRMATION ACTIVITY, children write down each other's unique, God-given qualities.

PREPARATION: You'll need a Bible, construction paper, and markers. The activity works best for older kids who read and write.

Gather kids in a circle and say: **It's always special to spend time with you because there's no other group of kids in the world exactly like you. Listen to what Psalm 139 says about how special each of you is.**

Read aloud Psalm 139:1-16. Then give each person a marker and a sheet of construction paper. Tell kids they'll have one minute to draw a self-portrait. Be sure you draw a self-portrait too. Have kids write their names underneath their portraits, then set their papers on the floor in front of them.

Then say: **When I say, "scooch left," everyone will move one space to the left. Then you'll have thirty seconds to write something nice about the person whose self-portrait is in front of you. Then I'll say, "scooch left," and we'll all move again. We'll keep going until we come back to our own portraits.** **Remember, write only positive, nice things. Here we go. Scooch left.**

When kids have moved all the way around the circle and returned to their own papers, allow time for them to read their classmates' comments. Then close with a prayer, thanking God for each child by name. Have kids keep their papers as reminders that God made each of them unique and wonderful.

Proverbs

"Trust the Lord with all your heart, and don't depend on your own understanding. Remember the Lord in all you do, and he will give you success."

Proverbs 3:5-6

PROVERBS 2:1-6

THEME:
Wisdom comes from God.

SUMMARY:
This bejeweled CRAFT helps kids learn the importance of remembering God's Word.

PREPARATION: You'll need a Bible; scissors; craft jewels in different sizes, colors, and shapes; tape; and tacky craft glue. Make photocopies of the "Treasure Box" pattern (p. 133) on heavy paper. You'll need one copy for each child. Make a sample treasure box using the directions on page 134.

Set out the supplies and the "Treasure Box" copies. Open your Bible to Proverbs 2:1-6 and say: **This Scripture passage talks about hunting for hidden treasure. Listen carefully and see if you can discover what that hidden treasure is.** Read the passage aloud, then ask:

● **What is the hidden treasure?**
● **Why is wisdom such a great treasure?**
● **Where can you find this treasure?**

Say: **The Bible is full of hidden treasure. It tells us what God is like, how God wants us to live, and how to handle difficult situations.** Ask:

● **Who can tell about some of the wise things the Bible teaches us?**

TREASURE BOX

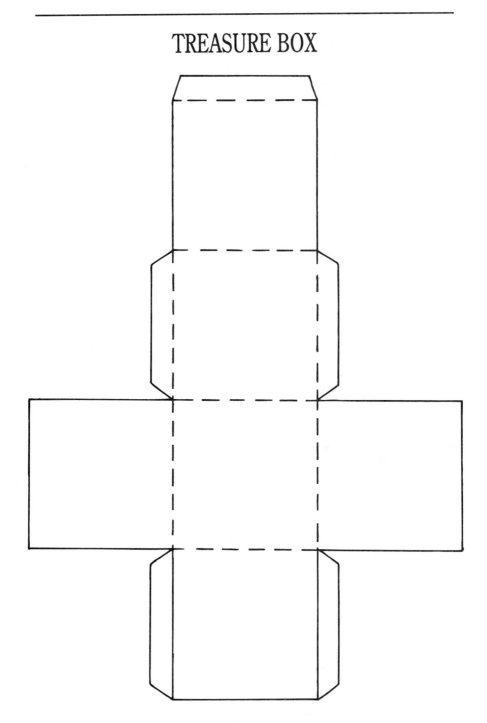

Allow several children to respond. Then say: **To celebrate God's treasure of wisdom that's found in the Bible, we're going to make treasure boxes.**

Show the sample box. Have kids cut out the box pattern on the heavy lines, fold on the dotted lines, and tape the tabs to the inside of the box. Then let each child choose a few craft jewels to glue to the top of his or her box. If you have extra time, let kids write favorite Bible verses onto slips of paper and tuck them inside their boxes.

Say: **Keep your treasure boxes as a reminder that the greatest treasure on earth is the wisdom that's found in God's Word!**

PROVERBS
6:6-11

THEME:
It's wise to work hard.

SUMMARY:
On this field TRIP, kids observe the industrious ways of ants and brainstorm ways to be hard-working in their own lives.

PREPARATION: You'll need a Bible. Each child will need a sack lunch and a drink. Plan to have one teenage or adult helper for every four or five kids. This is a fair-weather activity, so have a backup plan just in case.

Take a trip to a nearby park and enjoy a sack lunch with the kids. Encourage each child to save a few scraps of food. Have kids form groups of four or five, and assign each group a teenage or adult helper.

Say: **In just a moment, I'm going to send you out on an ant-finding expedition. When you find a group of ants, don't disturb them. Observe the ants carefully, and set out a few food scraps for them to find. Report back here in ten minutes to tell about what you discovered as you observed the ants.**

When kids return, ask:

● **What kinds of things did you see the ants doing?**

● **What did the ants do with the food you put out for them?**

Have someone read aloud Proverbs 6:6-11. Ask:

● **Why do you think ants work so hard?**

● **What does the Bible say we can learn from ants?**

Say: **In your groups, tell each other two ways you'll work hard at home and two ways you'll work hard at school.**

Have kids line up like ants as they march from the park.

PROVERBS 13:20

THEME:
God wants us to choose our friends wisely.

SUMMARY:
In this active DEVOTION, kids compare choosing a piece of candy to choosing friends.

PREPARATION: You'll need a Bible and a box of assorted chocolates.

EXPERIENCE
Ask:
● **What do you look for in a friend?**
Read aloud Proverbs 13:20, then ask:
● **What does the Bible tell us about choosing friends?**
Say: **God wants us to choose friends who are wise. To find out what wise friends are like, I'm going to have you finish a pop-up sentence. I'll say, "A wise friend is someone who . . ." and then you take turns popping up and finishing the sentence. I'd like to hear from *everyone!* Here we go. A wise friend is someone who . . .**
Each time a child pops up and finishes the sentence, repeat what the child said so everyone can hear. Continue repeating the pop-up sentence until most kids have responded.
Say: **You did such a great job with the pop-up sentence that I'd like to share a treat with you.** Pass around a box of assorted

chocolates. Encourage kids to take the first one they touch!

RESPONSE
As kids enjoy their chocolates, ask:
● **Did you get a chocolate that you really liked? Explain.**
● **How is choosing a chocolate like choosing a new friend?**
● **What can help you choose the right kind of friend?**

CLOSING
Pray: **Lord, please help us choose our friends carefully. Guide us to choose wise friends and to be wise friends. In Jesus' name, amen.**

PROVERBS 18:21

THEME:
Kind, careful speaking honors God.

SUMMARY:
This AFFIRMATION ACTIVITY helps kids discover how positive words give life.

PREPARATION: You'll need a Bible and a roll of masking tape. Lay a masking tape line down the middle of your room, then use the tape to make a large D (for Death) on the left half of the floor and a large L (for Life) on the right half of the floor.

Ask:
● **What's the most power-**

ful muscle in your body?

Say: I'd like to see you flex your most powerful muscle. Pause. Hmm—that's strange. The Bible says that a certain muscle holds the power of life and death, but no one flexed that muscle. Listen for the mystery muscle in Proverbs 18:21.

Read Proverbs 18:21 to the kids. Ask:

● What's the mystery muscle?

● Why is the tongue so powerful?

● How can our words bring life?

● How can our words mean death?

Say: Good, life-giving words encourage people and help them do their best. Mean words discourage people and make them feel like giving up. Our words don't actually kill people, but nasty talk can hurt people very badly. Let's see how that works. Find a partner, and stand facing each other across the masking tape line. I'll make a statement. The partner on the D side will say something mean or hurtful. The partner on the L side will respond with something kind and encouraging. For the next statement, switch sides. After each statement that follows, you'll switch sides again. Here we go.

Pause for kids to give their responses after each of the following statements.

● Your mom says, "I'm too tired to clean up the kitchen tonight. Could you help?

● Your friend says, "I can't believe I got such a bad grade in math."

● Your little sister says, "Would you play house with me?"

● Your neighbor says, "Please don't ride your bike across my lawn."

● Your dad says, "You may watch your program tomorrow. Today I'm going to watch this football game."

● Your older brother says, "Don't bug me—can't you see I'm busy?"

● Your friend says, "When you left me alone at lunch, it really hurt my feelings."

Gather kids in a circle and ask:

● What was it like when you said mean things?

● How did it feel to say positive things?

● When is it hard for you to say life-giving words?

● Why is it important to use life-giving words every day?

● How can you do that?

Say: Stand and face your partner once more. Affirm your partner with life-giving words, then we'll close in prayer.

Pause as kids affirm their partners, then pray: Lord, please help us remember how much power there is in what we say. Please fill our hearts with your love so we can say kind, encouraging words that give life. In Jesus' name, amen.

PROVERBS
23:22-25

THEME:
God wants us to listen to our parents.

SUMMARY:
With this creative MUSIC IDEA, kids share important things they've learned from their parents.

PREPARATION: You'll need a Bible.

Read aloud Proverbs 23:22-25. Say: **Turn to a partner, and tell about a time when it was hard to obey your parents.** Pause for kids to share. Then ask:
● **What makes it hard to obey your parents?**
● **When do you find it easy to obey your parents?**
● **Why do you think the Bible tells us that obeying parents is really important?**
Say: **When you learn to obey your parents, you're also learning to obey God. Parents try hard to teach habits and attitudes that will help you live a happy life.** Ask:
● **Who can tell about a time you ignored your parents' instructions and something bad happened?** You may want to share an experience from your own childhood to stimulate discussion.
● **Who can tell about a time you learned something really important from your mom or dad—something that helped**

you do the right thing?
Say: **Obeying parents isn't always easy, but it's always important. Let's learn a fun song to celebrate the good things we've learned from our moms and dads.**
Sing the following words to the tune of "This Old Man."

Mom and Dad, they taught me
To be the best that I can be.
They taught me how to listen and be kind
And to love Jesus all the time!

Have kids sing the song twice so they become familiar with the words. Then say: **When we sing the song this time, we'll pause after, "They taught me," and I'll point to four or five people. If I point to you, shout out something your parents taught you. After each person I point to has responded, we'll finish the verse. Then we'll start over and do the same thing.**
Repeat the song until all the kids have had a chance to shout something they've learned from their parents.

PROVERBS 27:2

THEME:
It's good to encourage each other.

SUMMARY:
Through this LEARNING GAME, kids discover that it's fun to give and receive praise.

PREPARATION: You'll need a Bible.

Say: We're going to play a game called Brag Tag. In this game, the only way we can move around is by shuffling backward. Both feet have to stay in contact with the floor at all times. I'll be "It" first. When I tag someone, everyone has to freeze. Then I'll brag and say nice things about the person I tagged. That person becomes It, and I sit down. Keep playing until everyone has tagged and bragged. Let's play!

After everyone has been tagged and bragged about, have kids sit in a circle. Read aloud Proverbs 27:2, then ask:

● What's wrong with bragging about ourselves?

● Why is it good to praise each other?

Say: Sometimes we think that if we accomplish great things, people will like us. For instance, pretend you were the best runner or artist or tuba player in your whole school. Ask:

● Would that make people like you? Why or why not?

● How do people feel about you if you're really good at something and you brag about it?

● How do people feel about you if you're really good at something but don't brag about it?

● How do people feel about you if you're not the best at anything, but you're friendly and kind?

Say: When we brag, we're trying to impress people. But what really happens is that other people feel put down. And putting people down won't win any friends! It's important to understand that people don't like you because of what you can *do*, but that people like you because of who you *are*! Ask:

● How can you be a person that people like?

Say: Remember, the best way to win friends is to *be* a friend. Now let's play one more round of Brag Tag to practice building people up.

ECCLESIASTES

"If people please God, God will give them
wisdom, knowledge, and joy."

Ecclesiastes 2:26a

ECCLESIASTES 3:1-8

THEME:
There is a time for everything.

SUMMARY:
This LEARNING GAME brings home the point that there is a time for everything—especially a time to laugh!

PREPARATION: You'll need a Bible.

Invite children to sit in a circle. Say: **The Bible tells us that there's a time for everything. As I read these verses from Ecclesiastes, see if you can count how** many different things the writer lists. Keep a careful count.

Read aloud Ecclesiastes 3:1-8, then ask:

● **How many things did you count?** (Twenty-eight.)

Say: **Right now it's time for us to laugh. I need a volunteer to be "It" and sit in the center of the circle.** When you have a volunteer, continue: **You can crawl up to anyone in the circle and ask, "Is it time to laugh?"** Use your funniest voice and facial expression to try to make the person laugh. The person you ask must pat you on the head and say, "No, it's not time to laugh" without cracking a smile. If that person smiles, he or she is It. If that person keeps a straight face, you can go to someone else. If three people answer you without smiling, the third person automatically becomes It.

Play until everyone has a chance to be It. Then say: **The next time you're sad, remember that God gives good times and hard times in our lives. The bad times aren't so bad when you know that good times are coming!**

ECCLESIASTES
7:5

THEME:
Accepting correction helps us learn and grow.

SUMMARY:
Use this active DEVOTION to help kids realize that receiving correction helps us grow.

PREPARATION: You'll need mini-marshmallows, aluminum pie pans, masking tape, and one blindfold for every three children. You'll also need newsprint, a watch with a second hand, and a Bible.

EXPERIENCE
Have children form groups of three and decide who's One, who's Two, and who's Three. Say: **Ones, your job is to toss minimarshmallows into pie pans. The problem is that you'll be wearing blindfolds.**

Twos, your job is to make the Ones feel good. You can say encouraging things such as "Way to go!" "Hang in there!" or "You can do it!" But don't give any specific instructions.

Threes, your job is to give the Ones helpful instructions. You might say, "Toss it a little harder," "A little farther to the right," or "Not quite so far."

Make sure kids understand their roles, then have trios spread out around the room. Give each trio a handful of marshmallows, a pie pan, and a blindfold. Have the Ones put on their blindfolds. Place a large sheet of clean newsprint under each pie pan, then lay a masking tape line three feet away from the pie pans.

Say: **We're going to play two rounds of this game. During the first round, only the Twos can talk to the Ones. The Threes can silently keep track of how many marshmallows land in the pan, collect the marshmallows, and hand them back to the Ones. I'll give you one minute to see how many marshmallows you can land in the pan. Ready? Go!**

Call time after one minute, and have each group report its score. Then say: **During this second round, only the Threes can talk. The Twos will silently keep score, collect the marshmallows, and hand them back to the Ones. You'll have one more minute. Go!**

After a minute call time, collect the blindfolds and pans, and let kids eat the marshmallows.

RESPONSE
Gather kids in a circle, and have each group report whether it scored more during the first or second round. It's likely that most groups did better in the second round with the Threes instructing

the Ones. Ask:

- **Why did most of the scores go up during the second round?**
- **Ones, what kinds of comments helped you?**
- **In real life, when do we need instruction and correction?**
- **Is it easy to receive correction? Why or why not?**

Say: **Listen to what the Bible says about receiving correction.** Read aloud Ecclesiastes 7:5. Ask:

- **Why is it important to accept correction?**
- **Who gives you correction and instruction? Why do they do that?**
- **How do you feel when someone corrects you?**

Say: **It's nice to receive encouragement like the Twos gave. But encouragement alone doesn't help us reach our goals. We need instruction and correction to help us learn to live our lives in ways that please God.** Hold up your Bible. **This book is full of stories about people who accepted correction and people who didn't. Wise people accept correction even if it's hard.**

CLOSING

Say: **Let's pray and thank God for the people who correct and instruct us.** Pray: **Lord, thank you for the people who care about us enough to correct us. Help us learn from them and grow. Thank you for all the wonderful instruction you give us in your Word. Amen.**

ECCLESIASTES 11:6

THEME:
God blesses our work for him.

SUMMARY:
In this SERVICE PROJECT, kids "tend God's garden."

PREPARATION: You'll need a Bible, gardening tools, bedding plants, and seeds or bulbs. Get permission to plant or spruce up flower beds around your church or at the home of an older person from your congregation.

If you do this service project in the spring or early summer, purchase a few bedding plants as well as seeds that start easily, such as marigolds, moss roses, or sweet alyssum. If you do it in fall, purchase bulbs such as tulips, daffodils, and grape hyacinths.

Gather children around the area where you've received permission to plant. Talk about the varieties of plants you've gathered, how tall they grow, whether they do well in sunlight or shade, and what kind of soil they need. Explain how important it is to plan a flower bed so the plants will thrive and look good together.

Let children take turns digging and planting. Then gather them around your planted flower bed, and read aloud Ecclesiastes 11:6.

Say: **We've worked hard to make a nice flower bed, but only God knows how it will turn out. Let's pray and ask God to** bless our work and help our flowers grow.

Close with a simple prayer. In the following weeks, point out how the flower bed is doing. Let kids take turns watering and weeding.

ECCLESIASTES 12:13-14

THEME:
God knows about "hidden" things.

SUMMARY:
This OBJECT LESSON shows kids the importance of "being real" with God and not trying to hide anything from him.

PREPARATION: You'll need wrapping paper, newspaper, scissors, and tape. Gather exciting and not-so-exciting gifts, such as a bag of treats, a package of stickers, a bag of fish-shaped crackers, an old shoe, a bottle of dishwashing detergent, and a box of fresh strawberries. You'll need one gift for every four students.

Before class, wrap all the gifts. Wrap some in plain newspaper and some in colorful wrapping paper. Make sure some of the exciting gifts are plainly wrapped and some of the less-exciting gifts are wrapped in fancy gift wrap. Display all the wrapped gifts on a table at the front of the room.

Have kids form groups of four. Ask each group to pick a gift. Before kids open their gifts, ask:

● **What do you think is inside your package?**

● **What made you decide to choose that package?**

Invite groups to open their gifts and show the other groups what they received. Ask:

● **Were you pleased or disappointed with what was inside your package? Explain.**

Have kids set their gifts aside as you read aloud Ecclesiastes 12:13-14. Ask:

● **What kinds of things do people try to hide from God?**

● **How is doing bad things in secret like hiding a yucky gift in a pretty package?**

● **Can anyone ever fool God the way I fooled some of you with fancy wrapping paper? Explain.**

● **If we do something wrong, what should we do instead of trying to hide it?**

Say: **When we do something wrong, let's not hide it. Let's confess it to God and ask him to forgive us and change us.**

Ask the kids who received the edible gifts to share their treats with everyone.

SONG OF SOLOMON

"He brought me to the banquet room, and his banner over me is love."

Song of Solomon 2:4

SONG OF SOLOMON 2:1-3

THEME:
God made each of us unique.

SUMMARY:
Use this AFFIRMATION ACTIVITY to help kids see how each of them is special.

PREPARATION: You'll need dill pickles, bread, cheese, apples, carrots, and gumdrops. Before class, prepare plates with bite-sized pieces of each of the foods. Cover the plates with napkins so the food is hidden. You'll also need a whole apple, a flower, and a Bible.

Have children find partners. Say: **We're about to enjoy a food-tasting party. Decide which partner will be the Eater and which will be the Feeder.** Have the Feeders tie blindfolds on the Eaters.

Uncover the plates of dill pickles, bread, and cheese. Tell the Feeders to use toothpicks to pick up a piece of food from one plate and feed it to the Eaters, who will then whisper their guesses about what they just tasted. Then have the Feeders and Eaters repeat the process with food from the other two uncovered plates.

After the Eaters have guessed about all three foods, have the Feeders and Eaters trade roles. Cover the dill pickles, bread, and cheese, and uncover the apples, carrots, and gumdrops. When kids have tasted and guessed all three foods, call everyone together. Ask:

● **Was it easy or hard to tell what the different foods were? Explain.**

Say: **Each of the foods you tasted had a unique flavor. The word "unique" means "one and only." Only dill pickles can taste like dill pickles, and you would never confuse the taste of dill pickles with chocolate cake! Just as the foods you tasted were unique, each of you is unique. God has made each of you special. It's the unique things about each of us that make us special to the important people in our lives.** Ask:

● **Who are some of the important people in your life?**

● **What are some of the special things they say they like about you?**

Say: **There's a book in the Bible that tells about a man and a woman who loved the special things about each other. In Bible times they said things differently than the way we do today. Listen for the way these two people tell what they appreciate about each other.**

As you read Song of Solomon 2:1-3 aloud, mention when it is the woman speaking and when it is the man. Expect a few giggles. Ask:

● **What were the compliments these people gave each other?**

● **Would you like to be called a lily or an apple tree? Why or why not?**

● **How do you tell people— your parents, for instance—that you appreciate the special things about them?**

● **How do you tell a friend that he or she is special?**

Say: **God made each of us unique and loves each of us individually.** Bring out a whole apple and a flower. **Let's have fun naming the unique things about each other. When I hand this apple to a guy, we'll all shout the special things we appreciate about him. When I hand this flower to a girl, we'll all shout the things we appreciate in her. All of our comments need to be kind and gentle.**

Toss the apple to a boy. Lead kids in shouting affirmations for about ten seconds. Then take the apple back, and hand the flower to a girl. After a few seconds of affirmations, take the flower back and hand the apple to another boy. Continue until all the kids have been affirmed.

Close with a prayer similar to this one: **Lord, thank you for this special group of kids, Thank you that you've made each of them as different and wonderful as dill pickles and gumdrops. Thank you that we all share the special gift of loving you. In Jesus' name, amen.**

SONG OF SOLOMON 2:11-13a

THEME:
God sends new life in spring.

SUMMARY:
Use this PARTY idea to celebrate the new life God sends each spring. (This would be a great party to hold on a cold January evening as a cure for the post-Christmas blahs!)

PREPARATION: You'll need party supplies as described below for the activities you choose.

As an icebreaker, have kids work together to make a "blooming" wall. Set out white paper plates, green crepe paper streamers, construction paper, scissors, glue sticks, masking tape, and markers. Challenge kids to make giant flowers using a paper plate as the center of each blossom and a green crepe paper streamer as the stem. They can glue construction paper petals to the paper plate centers. Before kids attach their flowers to the wall, have them get the autographs of five other kids on their paper plates. Encourage kids to tape their flowers to the wall at different heights so the decorated wall resembles a giant flower garden. Gather everyone in front of the finished wall, and read Song of Solomon 2:11-13a. Say: **We can celebrate God's special spring gifts any time of year!**

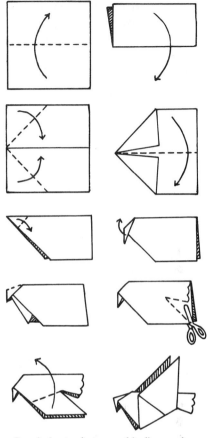

Permission to photocopy this diagram from *The Children's Worker's Encyclopedia of Bible-Teaching Ideas: Old Testament* granted for local church use. Copyright © Group Publishing, Inc., P.O. Box 481, Loveland, CO 80539.

Let kids make paper doves. Photocopy the step-by-step diagram above, and give a copy to each child. Demonstrate how to cut and fold the doves and explain that they'll fly like paper airplanes. Have kids see who can fly them the farthest.

Have some messy fun with egg-carton gardens. Cut egg cartons in half. Set out markers, potting soil, plastic spoons, different kinds of seeds, a watering pot, and plastic wrap. Have kids write their names on their egg cartons and then spoon potting soil into each cup and plant seeds of their choice. Encourage them to write on each cup the kind of seed that's planted in it. Help kids lightly water each cup and then cover their cartons with plastic wrap. Explain that they'll need to keep their egg-carton gardens in a warm, sunny spot and remove the plastic wrap when the first seeds sprout.

Use an instant-print camera for instant photo fun. Have kids form groups of five or six and arrange themselves in flower formations. For instance, they might arrange themselves in spokes like the petals of a daisy or form the leaves, stem, and cup of a tulip. Have kids make their funniest faces as you take their pictures.

Set out round sugar cookies and molasses cookies, gumdrops, licorice strips, pink- and white-coated licorice candies, M&M's, canned frosting, plastic knives, paper plates, and napkins. Have kids each make three colorful flower cookies using the ingredients you've set out. Encourage them to make each cookie slightly different. Admire the table full of flower cookies before kids gobble them up.

Isaiah

"A child has been born to us; God has given a son to us. He will be responsible for leading the people. His name will be Wonderful Counselor, Powerful God, Father Who Lives Forever, Prince of Peace."

Isaiah 9:6

ISAIAH
1:18

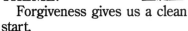

THEME:
Forgiveness gives us a clean start.

SUMMARY:
This CRAFT with tactile appeal helps kids understand that Jesus washes away their sins.

PREPARATION: You'll need newspaper, a Bible, several small mixing bowls, Ivory Snow soap flakes, measuring cups, tablespoons, and plastic sandwich bags.

Have kids form trios and sit together in circles. Give each trio a sheet of newspaper.

Say: **I'd like you to take turns telling each other about wrong things that kids do. When you name something, rub the palms of your hands on the newspaper. Take turns until each of you has named at least five wrong things that kids do.**

After kids have shared, ask:

● **What do your hands look like?**

● **How is that like the way we are on the inside after we've sinned and done wrong things?**

● **What does the Bible call the wrong things we do?**

Listen to what the Bible says we can do to get clean again. Read aloud Isaiah 1:18.

Say: **Jesus died for us on the cross so that our sins, the things that we do that are wrong, can** be washed away. **Let's make a neat craft as we find out what it's like to be forgiven and made clean again.**

Have kids gather around a table where you've set out the mixing bowls, soap flakes, measuring cups, and tablespoons. Have each trio measure and pour into a bowl one cup soap flakes and one tablespoon water. Have them take turns kneading the mixture and forming it into three balls. (Warn kids not to rub their eyes!)

When each trio has made three soap balls, ask:

● **What happened to the ink on your hands?**

Say: **Jesus can clean our hearts just as the soap cleans our hands.** Distribute the plastic bags, and have kids place their soap balls in the bags. **When you take your soap ball home, tell your family how Jesus' forgiveness makes our hearts as white as snow!**

Close with a prayer thanking Jesus for his wonderful gift of forgiveness.

ISAIAH
8:12-13

THEME:
God protects us because he loves us.

SUMMARY:
Use this OBJECT LESSON to help kids understand God's protection.

PREPARATION: You'll need a Bible, a sheet cake, birthday candles, matches, and a taper candle in a holder with a glass hurricane shade.

A sk:
● **When you were a little tiny kid, what were you afraid of?**

● **Now that you're older, what's the scariest thing in the whole world to you?**

Allow several of the kids to answer. Then say: **No matter what our fears might be, God is bigger and stronger than any of them. Listen to what the Bible says.** Read aloud Isaiah 8:12-13. **The prophet Isaiah was talking to the people of Israel about their powerful enemies. But Isaiah knew that God was the most powerful of all. Let's see how God's power compares to people's power.**

Set out the sheet cake and birthday candles. Have each child place a candle on the cake. Light the birthday candles and the taper candle. Replace the glass hurricane shade around the taper candle.

Say: **The birthday candles represent the power we have. Sometimes scary things happen, and the winds of trouble blow in our lives. Blow at these candles on the cake.** When all the candles have been blown out, say: **We're not very strong, are we? But God is like this candle.** Point to the taper candle. **Blow at this candle the same way you blew at the birthday candles.** Don't allow children to blow down the top of the hurricane shade. Ask:

● **Why didn't this candle go**

out?

Say: **God is more powerful than anything in the universe. When we trust in him, we don't need to be afraid. Now let's celebrate God's care for us and gobble up this cake!**

ISAIAH 53:4-6

THEME:

Jesus takes our weaknesses and gives us his strengths.

SUMMARY:

Use this OBJECT LESSON to show how Jesus gives us the best end of the deal in every exchange we make with him.

PREPARATION: You'll need a Bible, a small package of cookies for each child, and a dirty dust rag. Put the rag in a box, and wrap it with gift wrap.

Give each child a small package of cookies. Ask children to leave the packages unopened and to choose a partner. Ask the following questions, and have partners share their answers with each other. Hold up the wrapped box with the rag inside and ask:

● **What would make you want to trade your cookies for what's inside this box?**

● **What do you think might be in the box?**

Trade the box with a child who's willing to trade. Have the child hold up the rag. Ask the child:

● **Are you glad you made the trade? Why or why not?**

● **Would you like to trade again and get your cookies back?** Return the cookies to the child, then say: **The dirty dust rag wasn't a very good trade for a package of cookies.** (Name of child) **gave up something good and got something yucky in return. Did you know that's exactly what Jesus did for us. Listen.**

Read aloud Isaiah 53:4-6. Ask:

● **What did Jesus trade us for?**

● **What did Jesus give up in the trade?**

● **Why was Jesus willing to make that kind of trade?**

Pray: **Thank you, Jesus, for loving us enough to take our sin and pain and suffering and punishment and to give us your love in return. We love you. Amen.**

Let the kids enjoy their cookies.

ISAIAH 55:10-11

THEME:

God's Word is powerful.

SUMMARY:

This art and CRAFT project reminds kids that God's Word always bears fruit!

PREPARATION: You'll need a Bible, construction paper, markers, clear self-stick paper, scissors, glue sticks, and tape. Gather and place in separate containers your choice of the following pairs of items:

grass seed and blades of grass, acorns and leaves from an oak tree, tiny pine cones and pine needles, and flower seeds and blooming flowers. Cut the clear self-stick paper into two-by-two-inch squares.

Set out construction paper, markers, squares of clear self-stick paper, and containers of items you collected. Gather kids around the table and say: **God's Word, the Bible, is like seed. When we plant it in our hearts, it grows good things in our lives. Listen to how the prophet Isaiah explained it.** Read aloud Isaiah 55:10-11. **Let's do a fun art project to show how God's Word grows good things.**

Have each child take a sheet of construction paper, fold it in half, and open it again. Have each child write, "This seed" at the top of the left side of the paper and "grows this" at the top of the right side of the paper. Invite kids to place pairs of items from the containers in rows on their papers. For instance, they would place grass seed on the left side and blades of grass on the right side, then cover those items with the clear self-stick paper. Have them continue with tiny pine cones on the left and pine needles on the right, flower seeds on the left and petals of a flower on the right.

Finally have kids draw a Bible in the left column and things that symbolize growth in their lives in the right. Suggest ideas such as a heart to show God's love, a simple family picture to show obedience to parents, praying hands to show prayer, a gift box to show kindness, or a sketch to show how they help others. Invite older kids to print Isaiah 55:11 at the bottom of their papers.

JEREMIAH

" 'I say this because I know what I am
planning for you,' says the Lord. 'I have good
plans for you not plans to hurt you. I will give
you hope and a good future.' "

Jeremiah 29:11

JEREMIAH 1:4-9

THEME:
God's love is meant to be shared.

SUMMARY:
Use this AFFIRMATION ACTIVITY to help children see that they can touch others' lives with God's love.

PREPARATION: For each child you'll need a clean plastic grocery bag with handles and a plastic sandwich bag full of jelly beans. Have children wash and dry their hands before this activity.

Hand out grocery bags, and help children slip their arms into the handles of the bags and wear them as backpacks. Bigger kids can slip both handles of their bags over one shoulder.

Give each child a bag of jelly beans. Have children scatter around the room. Say: **We're about to have a jolly jelly bean giveaway! Your job is to give your jelly beans away by placing them in other people's backpacks. But only special people can give their jelly beans away. For instance, if I say, "People who are over five feet tall," then only people who are over five feet tall can give their jelly beans away. Everyone else has to freeze. As you slip a jelly bean into someone's backpack, say, "God loves you!"**

When it's your turn to give jelly beans away, you can give them to three to five people, but you can only give one jelly bean to each person. Do your best to make sure that everyone has lots of jelly beans by the end of the game. If you run out of jelly beans to give away, freeze until the game is over.

Call out the following categories of people to give away their jelly beans. Pause about twenty seconds before calling the next category. You can adapt the categories to work with your group of children.

● **People who are wearing blue.**

● **People who have shoes that tie.**

● **People who wear glasses.**

● **People who can wiggle their ears.**

● **People who are in second grade.**

● **People who are wearing red.**

● **People whose hair is in a ponytail.**

● **People who have shoes that don't tie.**

● **People with birthdays in December.**

● **People who have jelly beans left to give away.**

After the jelly bean giveaway, gather children in a circle on the floor. Ask a good reader to read Jeremiah 1:4-9 aloud. Then ask:

● **What does God want us to do?**

● **How was playing our game like obeying this Scripture?**

● **What can be scary about** telling people about God's love?

● **How can we conquer those fears?**

Say: **In our game, special people could give their jelly beans away. God has made each of you a special person who can share his love. We all know people who need to hear about God's love. Close your eyes and think about someone you know who needs to hear about God's love. When you've thought of someone, quietly say that person's first name.**

Say a brief prayer asking God to help children share God's love with the people they named. Then close by putting your hand on the shoulder of the person on your left and saying: (Name)**, you can share God's love!** Have children pass the affirmation around the circle.

JEREMIAH 1:17-19

THEME:
God protects us.

SUMMARY:
Use this DEVOTION to help children understand that our powerful God protects them when they stand up for what's right.

PREPARATION: You'll need Bibles, newspaper, and a watch with a second hand.

EXPERIENCE
Have children form two groups. If you have a large class, form

groups of six to eight. Give each group a small stack of newspaper.

Say: **Go around your group and take turns telling when it's hard or scary to stand up for what's right. For instance, you might say, "It's hard to stand up for what's right when all my friends are doing something bad" or "It's hard to stand up for what's right when someone who's bigger than I am is bullying me."** As you share, crumple a sheet of newspaper into a ball.

Allow two or three minutes for children to share, then clap your hands to get kids' attention. Designate one group as the Protectors and the other group as the Tossers.

Say: **Protectors, choose one person in your group to defend. That person will stand in the middle as you form a solid circle of protection by standing shoulder to shoulder around him or her, facing out. Tossers, when I say "go," you'll have fifteen seconds to toss your paper wads at the person in the middle of the Protectors. Protectors, you may wave your arms high in the air to deflect the paper wads, but you may not catch them—only bat them away.**

When children have formed their groups, shout, "Go!" Call time if a paper wad hits the protected person or when fifteen seconds have elapsed. If a paper wad touches the protected person, have groups switch places. If the protected person doesn't get hit, have that person join the circle and choose another teammate to stand in the middle. Play until all the children have had a turn being the protected person.

RESPONSE

Have children sit in their groups. Hand out Bibles, and have a volunteer in each group read aloud Jeremiah 1:17-19. Then ask the following questions, pausing after each one to give groups time for discussion:

● **Why does God tell us to not be afraid?**

● **How was being protected in our game like being protected by God?**

● **How was it different?**

● **When have you experienced God's protection?**

CLOSING

Have kids stand in one large circle holding their paper wads. Pray: **Lord, thank you for helping us stand up for what's right even when it's difficult. Please help us trust in your protection. In Jesus' name, amen.**

Have children toss their paper wads in the air and shout, "Yea, God!"

JEREMIAH
9:23-24

THEME:
God desires our praise.

SUMMARY:
Use this creative PRAYER to help children learn to praise God for their accomplishments.

PREPARATION: You'll need markers and a paper plate for each child.

Give each child a paper plate. Demonstrate how to fold the plate in half with the top side of the plate folded in. When the plate is folded this way, it will tend to pop open. Have children use markers to draw lips on the front edges of the plate, as shown.

Say: **Congratulations! You're all the proud owners of your very own talking lips. Actually, these are bragging lips. I'd like you to find a partner and see which of you can come up with the biggest brag. For instance, you might use your bragging lips to say, "My dog is so smart that he helps me with my math homework" or "I'm the fastest runner in my whole school." Make up the most outrageous bragging you can think of.**

Give children two or three minutes to brag, then call everyone together. Ask:

● **Who wants to share the funniest thing your partner bragged about?**

After several children have shared, say: **That was a bunch of wild bragging!** Ask:

● **How does it feel to brag about yourself or something that belongs to you?**

Say: **Let's see what the Bible tells us about bragging.** Read aloud Jeremiah 9:23-24. Ask:

● **What does the Bible say we should brag about?**

● **How can we do that?**

Say: **Let's change our bragging lips into praying and praising lips. For instance, if you bragged about your dog, you could say, "Thank you, Lord, for giving me a smart, wonderful dog." When you've thought of a way to "boast in the Lord," pop up and use your praying and praising lips to say it out loud.**

You may need to "prime the pump" by leading the sharing time with praises of your own. Encourage children to share more than one praise.

Close by using the praying and praising lips to sing this song to the tune of "Old MacDonald Had a Farm."

God is great and God is good.
I'll praise God every day.
And when I boast, I'll boast in the Lord,
And this is what I'll say:
God is awesome! God's the best!
I'll put God above all the rest!
God is great and God is good.
I'll praise God every day.

JEREMIAH
10:1-6

THEME:
Harvest is a time to celebrate God.

SUMMARY:
Plan a PARTY to celebrate the fall harvest and thank our living God for his provision.

PREPARATION: You'll need party supplies as described below for the activities you choose to do.

Have a happy harvest party! Invite children to come dressed in old clothes and to wear silly hats. As children arrive, have them tear paper leaves from yellow, orange, and red construction paper and tape the leaves to lengths of twine to form garlands. Help children decorate the room with their garlands.

Form groups of four or five. Give each group a bag containing an old pair of jeans, a flannel shirt, a pair of old shoes, a balloon, an old hat, and a stack of newspapers. Have each group use the items to create a scarecrow, using the balloon for a head. Have kids set their finished scarecrows on chairs arranged along one wall.

Hand out sheets of construction paper and markers to children who finish their scarecrows first. Have children letter the words of Jeremiah 10:6 on construction paper, one word per sheet. Help children tape the words of the verse together in order. Then set the finished verse on the laps of the scarecrows.

Gather children in front of the scarecrows, and read aloud Jeremiah 10:1-6. Explain that in Old Testament times, Jewish people worshiped our living God who could not be seen. Other nations worshiped idols they made. Ask:

● **Would you ever want to pray to or worship one of our scarecrows? Why or why not?**

● **How is our God different from gods made of wood or stone or newspaper?**

● **What does God provide for us this time of year that you're especially thankful for?**

Tell children that in Bible times, Jewish people celebrated the harvest with dances and feasting. Play a cassette or CD of lively praise music and teach children a simple circle dance.

Set up fun games for kids to enjoy such as bobbing for apples, running relays with spoonfuls of pumpkin seeds, and passing ears of corn between their knees. For treats, have kids make their own cornucopias by filling sugar cones with candy corn and peanuts.

Join hands with kids in a circle, and have them share simple sentence prayers of thanks for all the wonderful blessings God gives us.

JEREMIAH
10:12-13

THEME:
God's power is awesome.

SUMMARY:
In this OBJECT LESSON, children create a "storm" and discuss God's incredible power.

PREPARATION: You'll need a Bible, two box fans, black plastic garbage bags, newspaper, spray bottles of water, and flashlights. You'll also need noisemakers such as pots and pans and wooden spoons.

Say: Today we're going to create a storm to celebrate God's power. Before we begin, I'd like you to tell me about the most powerful thing you've ever seen. Let several children respond, then read about God's power from Jeremiah 10:12-13.

Choose two dependable, older children to operate the box fans. Give some children the plastic bags to stuff with crumpled newspaper and then to wave as storm clouds. Give some children the spray bottles to use to shoot water in the air (not at each other). Give some children flashlights to create lightning. Let the rest of the children choose pans and wooden spoons to bang together to make thunder.

When everyone is ready with their props, dim the lights in your room and shout: **Let the storm begin!** Then let the storm rage for thirty seconds to a minute. Stop the storm by turning up the lights.

Have children set their props in a corner of the room and then gather in a circle. Ask:

● **What words can you think of to describe God's power?**

● **How does it feel to serve such a powerful God?**

● **When have you seen God's power at work in your life?**

● **When is it important to remember how powerful God is?**

Close by allowing kids to create a storm once more as they sing "Awesome God."

JEREMIAH 15:16

THEME:
God's Word is worth sharing.

SUMMARY:
Use this creative PARTY idea to get kids enthused about learning and sharing God's Word.

PREPARATION: You'll need party supplies as described below for the activities you choose.

Before children arrive, make delicious peanut butter dough by mixing nearly equal parts of peanut butter and powdered sugar and a few drops of vanilla. Add and stir in the powdered sugar until the dough is firm and loses its stickiness.

As children arrive, have them form groups of six. Give each group a lump of peanut butter dough, a sheet of wax paper, and plastic sandwich bags to slip over their hands. Have each group choose a well-known Bible story and work together to model characters from the dough to tell that story. When groups are ready, have them present their stories to each other. After the story presentations, give each group a hearty round of applause. Then tell kids to gobble up the dough!

Then say: **We just did something the prophet Jeremiah did!** Read aloud Jeremiah 15:16 using the New International Version. Discuss the meaning of the verse, then tell kids you'll have lots of fun "eating up" God's Word at this party.

Set out bowls of alphabet cereal, and invite children to work with partners and use the cereal to spell out a phrase from a favorite Bible verse, such as Psalm 23:1; John 3:16; or 1 John 4:7. If you have non-readers, be sure to pair them with older children. Invite children to gobble up the completed phrases.

Give each child a cup of alphabet soup. Invite children to arrange the letters they find in their soup to form the names of favorite Bible characters and then slurp their soup.

Bake a giant cookie on a pizza pan. Write, "God's Kids" with decorative frosting in the middle of the cookie. Invite children to autograph the cookie using a tube of frosting. After all the kids have written their names, let each child break off his or her name and eat it.

Close by singing "Thy Word."

JEREMIAH 17:7-8

THEME:
We can trust God.

SUMMARY:
On this field TRIP to a stream or river, children learn to give their worries to God.

PREPARATION: You'll need a small warmer candle and a small plastic foam meat tray or an aluminum potpie pan for each child.

You'll also need matches and a Bible. Plan to take children to a small stream just after sunset.

TEACHER TIP
Plan to have extra adult helpers to make sure children don't go into the water. Have another adult leader downstream from the group to gather the candles as they float by.

Give each child a candle to hold. Light your candle and read aloud Jeremiah 17:7-8. Then have children form trios and take turns finishing the sentence, "I sometimes worry about..."

After children have shared, let them come to you one by one, light a candle from yours, set it on the foam tray, and gently push the tray into the current of the stream.

Have all the children watch silently as their candles drift away. Encourage them to think of how God promises to take care of our worries. Close by quietly singing "God Is So Good."

JEREMIAH
18:3-6

THEME:
God shapes us as we are obedient.

SUMMARY:
Use this CRAFT project to help kids understand that God wants to mold and shape them into people he can use to build his kingdom.

PREPARATION: You'll need self-hardening clay, wax paper, pencils, twine, and aluminum pop cans. You'll also need a Bible and access to leaves. Before this activity, cut the wax paper into eight-inch squares.

TEACHER TIP

If you use unopened pop cans, you can enjoy the pop later as a treat. If you choose to use empty cans, tape over the openings to safeguard against cuts.

Give each child an egg-sized lump of clay, a pop can, two sheets of wax paper, a pencil, and an eight-inch length of twine.

Demonstrate how to place the clay between the sheets of wax paper and roll it flat with the pop can until the clay is about one-fourth inch thick. Have children look around outside for a leaf or sprig that will fit on their clay. Have each child place the leaf on the clay and under the top sheet of wax paper. Show children how to gently roll the pop can over the wax paper, creating a leaf impression in the clay.

Gather children in a circle with their clay pieces in front of them. Read aloud Jeremiah 18:3-6. Ask:

● **What did you do to make your clay piece look the way you wanted it?**
● **How does God shape us to be the way he wants us to be?**
● **What's good about letting God shape us?**
● **Why can we trust God to shape our lives the right way?**

Have each child use the point of a pencil to make a hole near the top of the clay. Explain that when the clay dries, the twine can be slipped through the hole and tied to make a hanger. Encourage children each to lay the clay on a flat surface at home where it can dry undisturbed for about twenty-four hours.

Pray: **God, help us to let you shape our lives. We want to be just like this clay to let you do your work in us. Thanks for wanting to shape us into special people. We love you. In Jesus' name, amen.**

JEREMIAH
23:23-24

THEME:
God is with us everywhere.

SUMMARY:
Use this LEARNING GAME to teach children that no one can hide from God.

PREPARATION: You'll need a large area with good hiding places.

You'll also need a special treat and a Bible.

Tell children they're going to play a backward game of Hide-and-Seek. In this game only one person hides and everyone else is "It." All the Its travel separately, looking for the one person who is hidden. Whoever finds the hidden person hides with him or her. Whoever finds those two, hides with them, and so on until everyone is hidden in the same spot. The last person to find the hidden group becomes the person who hides to begin the next round.

After two or three rounds, have children go to another room with an adult helper. Hide the special treat, and then invite children back into the room. Gather children and say: **I have one more thing for you to find. There's a treat hidden somewhere in this room.** After children find the treat, let them enjoy it. Ask:

● **What was fun about this game?**

● **What's the best hiding place you ever found while playing a game of Hide-and-Seek?**

● **Do you think God could find you there? Why or why not?**

Have a volunteer read aloud Jeremiah 23:23-24.

● **What kinds of things do people try to hide from God? Why?**

● **Why is it good that God can always see us?**

Close with a prayer of thanks to God for his watchful care.

JEREMIAH 29:11-13

THEME:
The future is in God's hands.

SUMMARY:
In this AFFIRMATION ACTIVITY, children learn that God has special plans for their lives.

PREPARATION: You'll need a Bible, a chair draped with fabric to form a throne, and a twelve-inch length of tinsel garland taped in a circle to form a crown.

Have children form a circle around the throne. Say: **The Bible has exciting news for God's people.** Read aloud Jeremiah 29:11-13. **Isn't that great? We don't know how our lives will turn out, but God does! Let's celebrate the wonderful future God has in store for each of us.**

Have the child to your left sit on the throne. As you place the crown on his or her head, say: (Name)**, God has good plans for you!** Then have the rest of the children say, "Search for God with all your heart!" and give that child a standing ovation. Have that child give you the crown and join the circle as the next child sits on the throne. Repeat the affirmation for all the children in the class.

JEREMIAH 31:3

THEME:
God's love is forever.

SUMMARY:
This wearable CRAFT project helps remind kids of God's abiding love.

PREPARATION: Place different-colored fabric paint in separate pie pans, and thin the paint slightly with fabric painting medium. You'll need newspaper, cardboard, paper towels, and a blow-dryer. You'll also need a prewashed T-shirt for each child. Be sure kids wear old clothes for this activity.

Show children how to stamp heart shapes by making fists with both hands, dipping the sides of their fists into fabric paint, and stamping them side by side onto newspaper. Or let them use heart halves cut from sponges. Encourage kids to use different colors for the two halves of each heart. Have kids practice stamping on the newspaper. Then demonstrate how to slip the cardboard into a T-shirt so that the paint doesn't bleed to the other side. Let children stamp hearts all over their shirts. Blow-dry the painted T-shirts.

TEACHER TIP
If the brand of fabric paint you use suggests heat-setting, tell children to ask their parents to put the painted shirts in their clothes dryers for about ten minutes.

Have kids read Jeremiah 31:3 together. Then ask:
- **What does it mean to us that God will love us forever?**
- **How can we thank God for this promise to always love us?**

Pray with kids, asking God for help to be thankful for his love and incorporating kids' suggestions into your prayer.

JEREMIAH 32:17

THEME:
We can praise God with music.

SUMMARY:
With this MUSIC IDEA, children use unique instruments to praise God.

PREPARATION: You'll need a CD or cassette player, a recording of "Ah, Lord God," newspaper, rubber bands, scissors, and your choice of materials listed below for making musical instruments.

Form two groups, the Music Makers and the Movers 'n' Shakers. Give the Music Makers a variety of interesting items to use to make musical instruments. You may want to include cardboard tubes, paper plates, dry beans, uncooked rice, round oatmeal containers, wooden spoons, ribbon, tape, combs, wax paper, glitter glue, and a stapler. Encourage children to make the most creative instruments they can think of.

Give the Movers 'n' Shakers newspaper, scissors, and rubber bands. Demonstrate how to make shakers by fringing sheets of newspaper into one-inch strips that stop three inches from the bottom. Show them how to roll the newspaper and secure the bottom with a rubber band. Let the Movers 'n' Shakers listen to the recorded song and make up interpretive motions with their shakers.

Finally bring the Music Makers and the Movers 'n' Shakers together, and let them perform the song together. Read aloud Jeremiah 32:17, and explain that it feels good to praise God because that's what God made us to do! Have them sing the song together one more time to wrap up the activity.

LAMENTATIONS

" 'But I have hope when I think of this: The Lord's love never ends; his mercies never stop.' "

Lamentations 3:21-22

LAMENTATIONS 3:21-26

THEME:
Patient prayer lets God work.

SUMMARY:
In this QUIET REFLECTION, children focus on God's faithfulness and on being patient in prayer.

PREPARATION: You'll need Bibles, paper, pencils, a cassette or CD player, and recorded instrumental worship music. You'll also need to make salt dough by mixing two cups flour, one cup salt, and a scant cup of water. Knead the dough until it's smooth and loses its stickiness.

Have kids form trios. Give each trio a pencil, a sheet of paper, and a Bible with a bookmark in the book of Lamentations. Have each group choose a Reader, a Writer, and a Reporter. Have the Readers read aloud Lamentations 3:21-26. Say: **I'd like you to think about all the things God faithfully gives you each day. We'll see which group has the longest list after three minutes.** Have the Writers jot down the ideas. Then call on the Reporters to read the lists aloud.

Then say: **The passage you read talks about hope and waiting patiently on the Lord. I'd like you to think about something you've been praying about for a long time or a hope that you have for the future.**

In a moment, I'll give you

each a lump of dough. Use the dough to model something that reminds you of what you're praying about or hoping for. For instance, if you're praying about a job for someone, you might form the dough into a dollar sign to represent the money the person would make in that job. If you're hoping that someone who is sick or sad will soon feel better, you could form the dough into a sun or a smiley face to represent a happier time.

Give each child a fist-sized lump of modeling dough. Play soft worship music as children work. Circulate among children and offer help and suggestions as needed. If some have trouble thinking of a prayer concern, share a concern from your church.

After two or three minutes, stop the music, and invite children to share their prayer concerns and hopes. Close with a prayer, thanking God for his faithfulness. Encourage children to keep their dough figures as prayer reminders.

EZEKIEL

" I will give them a desire to respect me completely, and I will put inside them a new way of thinking. I will take out the stubborn heart of stone from their bodies, and I will give them an obedient heart of flesh.' "

Ezekiel 11:19

EZEKIEL 1:22-28; 3:12

THEME:
God's glory is amazing.

SUMMARY:
Use this creative MUSIC IDEA to help children understand the glory of God.

PREPARATION: You'll need a Bible, silver tinsel garland, scissors, white tissue paper, and masking tape. You'll also need a cassette or CD player and a recording of the song "Our God Reigns" or another favorite praise song.

Have children gather in a large group. Say: **God gave the** prophet Ezekiel a vision of God's heavenly throne. Close your eyes as I read from the Bible what Ezekiel said about his vision. Read aloud Ezekiel 1:22-28; 3:12. Then ask:

● **How would you have felt if you'd had a vision like that?**

● **What do you think it would be like to see God's throne surrounded by angels?**

Say: **Let's make angel wings. Then we'll wear our wings as we sing a praise song about God's glory.**

Have kids form pairs and help each other cut two lengths of garland that extend from shoulders to wrists. Give each pair four sheets of white tissue paper. Have partners work together to gather and tape the tissue paper to the tinsel garland and then tape the finished "wings" to each other's arms.

Play "Our God Reigns," and encourage children to flap their wings as they praise the Lord.

EZEKIEL 36:24-29

THEME:
Forgiveness is a free gift.

SUMMARY:
Use this creative PRAYER to help kids appreciate God's wonderful gift of forgiveness.

PREPARATION: Gather charcoal briquettes, towels, and a dishpan of warm, soapy water. You'll also need a Bible, a cassette or CD player, and a cassette or CD of quiet music. Have children wear old clothes for this activity.

Have kids form trios. Give each trio a charcoal briquette. Say: **You'll each have a turn to hold the charcoal. When it's your turn, rub it between your hands as you think about something you did last week that you feel** bad about. For instance, you might have yelled at your mom, said bad things about someone, or said something that wasn't true. After you've thought of something, pass the charcoal to another person in your group.

Play soft music as children think quietly and pass the charcoal in their trios. Then collect the briquettes, turn off the music, and ask:

● **What's it like to think about bad things you've done?**

● **How is the charcoal on your hands like what you're feeling on the inside?**

Say: **I have good news! Listen to what God told the prophet Ezekiel to say to the people of Israel.** Read aloud Ezekiel 36:24-29. Then ask:

● **What does God say he will do?**

● **What does God want us to do?**

Invite trios to come and wash their hands in the warm, soapy water. As you dry each child's hands, say: (Name), **God is always willing to forgive you.** After all the children have washed their hands, pray: **Dear Lord, thank you for forgiving us and making us clean. In Jesus' name, amen.**

DANIEL

" 'But even if God does not save us,
we want you, O king, to know this:
We will not serve your gods or worship
the gold statue you have set up.' "

Daniel 3:18

DANIEL 3:1-30

THEME:
God wants us to stand up for what is right.

SUMMARY:
Use this CREATIVE STORYTELLING idea to impress kids with the courage of Shadrach, Meshach, and Abednego.

THE FIERY FURNACE

● Pile two or three chairs on top of each other to represent the golden statue.

● Choose one child to be the king, and have him stand proudly with his nose in the air and his arms crossed. Have the king point to the statue when you give the signal.

● Choose two or three children to be musicians and "trumpet" through cupped hands when you give the signal.

● Choose three children to be Shadrach, Meshach, and Abednego. Have them stand up straight, link arms, and shake their heads "no" when you give the signal.

● Have the rest of the children kneel in a semicircle to form the fiery furnace. Have them wave their arms in the air like flames when you give the signal.

When all the children are in place, read the following story.

King Nebuchadnezzar of Babylon was a very proud man. He built a huge golden statue ninety feet high. When the music

played *(signal the king and the musicians)*, the king ordered everyone to bow down to the statue. But when the music played *(signal the king and the musicians)*, Shadrach, Meshach, and Abednego *(signal them)* refused to bow down. They would worship no one but God.

Some troublemakers told the king that Shadrach, Meshach, and Abednego wouldn't bow to the golden statue. So the king summoned the three men to come to him.

"Is it true that you won't worship my statue?" the king demanded. "If you don't bow down when the music plays *(signal the musicians)*, I'll have you thrown into a fiery furnace *(signal the furnace)*.

Shadrach, Meshach, and Abednego *(signal them)* shook their heads. "We will worship no one but God," they answered. "God is able to save us."

The king became furious. "Throw them into the fire!" he commanded. "And heat it seven times hotter than usual." *(Signal the furnace.)*

Into the flames went Shadrach, Meshach, and Abednego The fire raged and roared *(signal the furnace)*. But Shadrach, Meshach, and Abednego didn't burn up! God sent an angel to protect them!

"Come here!" shouted the king. So Shadrach, Meshach, and Abednego came out of the fire and stood before the king.

Everyone listened in hushed silence as the king said, "Praise the God of Shadrach, Meshach, and Abednego, for he has sent his angel to rescue them. Now let everyone know that no one may say anything against their God!"

After the story, ask:
● **What did the three friends do that pleased God?**
● **What can we do to please God the way Shadrach, Meshach, and Abednego did?**

DANIEL
6:1-28

THEME:
God is faithful.

SUMMARY:
Use this CREATIVE STORYTELLING idea to retell the story of Daniel in the lions' den.

BRAVE DANIEL

As you tell this story, have kids listen for the following cue words and do the accompanying motions when they hear the words. Pause briefly for children's responses after each underlined word.
● Daniel—Say, "A brave, faithful man!"
● Daniel's enemies—Rub hands together and say, "Mean and nasty, mean and nasty!"
● lions—Roar loudly.

<u>Daniel</u> was one of the king's most trusted advisors. <u>Daniel's enemies</u> were jealous. "There must be a way to get rid of him," they thought. "Let's come up with a plan." And that's just

what they did. Daniel's enemies knew that Daniel prayed to God three times a day. So they went to the king and said, "O king, let's make a law that says people may only pray to you for the next thirty days. If people pray to anyone else, they will be thrown into a den of lions."

The king thought that sounded like a good law, so he signed it. Daniel's enemies cackled with glee. They waited until it was time for Daniel to pray. And sure enough, Daniel knelt right by his open window and prayed to God.

Then Daniel's enemies went to the king and said, "O king, we saw Daniel praying to his God. Now according to the law you signed, he must be thrown into a den of lions!"

The king felt very sad. He knew Daniel's enemies had tricked him. As Daniel was lowered into the den of lions, the king called out, "May your God save you!"

Daniel stayed all night in the den of lions. At first light, the king rushed to the den of lions. "Has your God been able to save you?" he shouted. Daniel answered, "Yes, O king, my God sent his angel to close the mouths of the lions."

The king clapped his hands with joy and gave an order for Daniel to be lifted out of the den of lions. Then he ordered Daniel's enemies to be thrown in the den of lions. And the king honored Daniel and God!

After the story, ask:
● Do you think you would have been brave enough to pray the way Daniel did? Why or why not?
● What do you think helped Daniel be brave?
● How does God help us be strong for him today?

HOSEA

" 'Come, let's go back to the Lord.' "

Hosea 6:1a

HOSEA 11:1-4

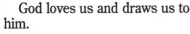

THEME:
God loves us and draws us to him.

SUMMARY:
In this CRAFT project, children make "ropes of love" to remind them of God's love.

PREPARATION: You'll need small bowls, liquid food coloring, old tube socks, scissors, a plastic tablecloth, and paint shirts or paint smocks. You can make simple paint smocks by cutting head and arm holes in paper grocery bags. You'll also need a Bible.

Before this activity, prepare food-coloring mixtures. Put a cup of water in each bowl. Stir in enough food coloring to make a dark colorful mixture. Make at least one bowl of colored water for every three children.

Give each child a tube sock. Demonstrate how to cut a sock into one-inch rings. This requires sharp scissors. For younger children, it's best to cut the socks ahead of time.

To make the ropes, stretch one ring into a circle, and lay it on the floor or tabletop. Stretch another ring into a circle and lay it to the right of the first ring with the edges overlapping slightly. Tuck the overlapping edge underneath the lower circle and then pull it up through the circle on the right. Pull tight, and the two circles will be linked together. Add the rest of the rings to the rope in the same fashion.

Set the bowls of food coloring on a plastic-covered table. Have children put on paint smocks and take turns dipping their ropes into the bowls of coloring. It's not necessary for children to soak the ropes with the coloring—just to touch them to the surface of the liquid. The color will spread through the cloth and bleed, making the ropes look tie-dyed.

When the children are finished, set the ropes aside to dry. Say: **The Bible says that God used ropes to tell people about his love. Listen to what the Bible says.**

Read aloud Hosea 11:1-4. Ask:

● **Why did the people wor-** **ship fake gods even though they knew God loved them?**

● **How do you think God felt when the people left him?**

● **How did God draw people back to himself?**

● **What do you think cords of human kindness and ropes of love are?**

● **How does God's love draw you to God?**

Have children take home their ropes to remind them of God's love and how it draws us close to God.

TEACHER TIP
You may want to have children take their damp ropes home in plastic bags.

JOEL

" 'After this, I will pour out my Spirit on all kinds of people.' "

Joel 2:28a

JOEL 2:12-13

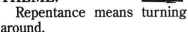

THEME:
Repentance means turning around.

SUMMARY:
In this LEARNING GAME, children determine whether their classmates are sincere.

PREPARATION: You'll need a Bible and a jar filled with bubble gum.

Choose one child to be the Judge and have him or her sit at a table. Set the jar of bubble gum on the table. Have the Judge choose two contestants to stand in front of the table. Instruct the Judge to turn around while you secretly give one of the two contestants a piece of bubble gum. Have both contestants hold their hands behind their backs.

Let the Judge turn around. Then give the contestants thirty seconds to convince the Judge that they need a piece of bubble gum. After thirty seconds call time, and have the Judge decide who should get the piece of bubble gum.

If the Judge chooses the contestant who didn't have a piece of bubble gum, then the Judge hands over the bubble gum and that child becomes the new Judge.

If the Judge chooses the child who already had a piece of bubble gum, then he or she remains the Judge for another round.

Play until everyone has stood

before the Judge.

Then read aloud Joel 2:12-13. Ask:

● In our game, what was it like trying to decide which person should get the bubble gum?

● In real life, is it easy to tell if people are sincere? Why or why not?

● Why is it important for us to be sincere when we turn away from our sins?

● How can we show God that we're sincere?

Say: **It was tough in this game to know who was sincere and who was trying to get a second piece of gum. But God always knows when we're sincere. We can't fool God. God knows when we're truly sorry for what we've done. To truly repent of the wrong we do, we must be willing not only to say we're sorry, but to stop doing wrong things. When we're sincere, God is always willing to forgive us.**

Amos

" The kingdom of David is like a fallen tent,
but in that day I will set it up again and
mend its broken places. I will rebuild its
ruins as it was before.' "

Amos 9:11

AMOS
5:24

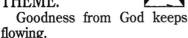

THEME:
Goodness from God keeps flowing.

SUMMARY:
This active DEVOTION helps children discover that God's goodness is unstoppable.

PREPARATION: You'll need several pitchers of water or a garden hose, newsprint, and markers. You'll also need towels and a Bible. Plan to do this devotion outside on a hot day. If you do it inside, set up a small inflatable wading pool in your room.

EXPERIENCE
Say: **I'm going to pour water into your hands. Your job is to try to keep any water from hitting the floor. Here we go.**
Pour water over each child's hands. Of course, it will be impossible to keep most of the water from hitting the ground. Pass around towels and have children dry their hands.

RESPONSE
Gather children away from the wet area. Ask:
● **Why couldn't you keep the water from hitting the ground?**
Say: **The Bible talks about a stream that never stops. Listen to Amos 5:24.** Have a volunteer read aloud Amos 5:24. Ask:
● **What is goodness?**
● **Where does goodness**

come from?

● **How is God's goodness like a stream that never stops?**

● **Can goodness come from us? What kinds of good things can we do?**

CLOSING

Say: **Let's become like a never-ending stream of goodness and brainstorm as many good things as we can.**

Ask children to stand in two rows facing each other, hold their hands out at waist level, and wiggle their fingers. Say: **Look—our hands have become a rippling stream. Let's take turns calling out good things we can do.**

After each child has told one good thing he or she can do, close with a prayer similar to this one: **God, help us to do good things for others. Help us make goodness flow like a stream that never stops. Help us to remember the good things you do for us and to give you praise. Amen.**

AMOS
7:7-9

THEME:
God alone is righteous.

SUMMARY:
This OBJECT LESSON shows children that no one "measures up."

PREPARATION: You'll need shelf paper, scissors, pencils, string, large paper clips, fine sandpaper, and chalk. The powdered chalk that

mountain climbers and gymnasts use works well, but you can also use sticks of chalk. Use the sandpaper to roughen the chalk so the chalk powder will stick to the string. Be sure you have a Bible on hand.

Before this activity, hang shelf paper on the wall in strips that are as tall as the children.

Form pairs, and have each pair stand by a strip of paper. Give each person a pencil.

Say: **Draw a line from the floor to the top of the paper. Make your line absolutely straight.**

Give the children a moment to draw their lines. Then say: **Now let's see how straight your lines are.**

Give each pair a piece of string that's as long as the height of the taller partner, several large paper clips, and a piece of colored chalk. Have each pair tie the paper clips to one end of the string. Then have pairs rub the colored chalk all over the string.

Have one partner hold the string against the paper with the paper clips hanging at the bottom of the string. After the string stops swinging, have the second partner hold the bottom of the string taut against the wall. Have them carefully snap it like a bowstring against the wall to create a chalk mark. Ask kids to compare the chalk lines to the pencil lines.

Read aloud Amos 7:7-9 and say: **A plumb line is what builders use to tell a straight wall from a crooked wall. You just created a plumb line with the string, the paper clip weights, and the chalk.** Ask:

● When God says he uses a plumb line to tell how crooked the people are, what does he mean?

● What happened when you compared the lines you drew to the chalk line? Explain.

● Why do our lives end up being a little crooked?

● If God wants us to live straight and perfect lives, what can we do?

Say: It's impossible for us to live up to God's measure of perfection. You all tried hard to draw straight lines, but they were still crooked. Even the person who lives the most careful life will still mess up sometimes. But when God forgives us, he straightens us out!

Pray: God, please forgive us for the bad things we do. We can't make our lives measure up, but your forgiveness straightens us out. Thank you for helping and forgiving us. We love you. Amen.

OBADIAH

"Your pride has fooled you."

Obadiah 3a

OBADIAH 3-4

THEME:
Pride can cause a fall.

SUMMARY:
This active DEVOTION demonstrates that pride is often a person's downfall.

PREPARATION: You'll need a Bible, blocks, and several small dolls or action figures.

EXPERIENCE

Form groups of three. Give each group a pile of blocks and a doll or action figure. Announce that kids have one minute to build the tallest tower they can build. After a minute call time, and challenge each group to balance its doll or action figure on top of the tower. Ask:

● **How would you feel if you were in the doll's place—on top of a tall tower like this one?**

● **What's likely to happen to this doll?**

If the towers fall, ask:

● **Why did the towers fall?**

● **What would have happened to the dolls if they'd been real people?**

RESPONSE

Say: **There's a passage in the Bible that talks about falling from a high place. Let's read it.**

Have a volunteer read aloud Obadiah 3-4. Ask:

● **We usually think of pride as a positive thing. When is it bad to be proud?**

● How is having this kind of pride like living on top of a shaky tower?

● Instead of having too much confidence in ourselves, who should we have confidence in? Explain.

● How will having confidence make our lives secure?

CLOSING

Have all the children work in one group to build a new tower with a broad, secure foundation. For each block they use, have them mention one way to build the foundation of their lives on God.

JONAH

" 'I [Jonah] knew that you are a God who is kind and shows mercy. You don't become angry quickly, and you have great love. I knew you would choose not to cause harm.' "

Jonah 4:2b

JONAH 1-4

THEME:
Quick obedience pleases God.

SUMMARY:
This LEARNING GAME teaches children the consequences of disobedience.

PREPARATION: You'll need masking tape, index cards, markers, and a treat such as brownies. You'll also need twenty items to use as landmarks such as books, shoes, balls, and other common classroom items.

Clear a large open space in your room by pushing the furniture against the walls. If your room is small, play this game in a fellowship hall or outside. Cover the floor with twenty parallel masking tape lines about one foot apart. The lines should extend from wall to wall. Put one of the landmark items at the end of each line. At one side of the room place a chair with the treat on it.

Give each child an index card. Have kids write their names and the letter O on one side of their cards. Have them write the letter D on the other side.

Determine which tape line is in the middle. Have children spread out along that line and face the treat.

Say: **The D on your card stands for disobey. The O on your card stands for obey. I'll read a list of instructions. Then you'll throw your card in the air. If the card lands on the O, you'll** obey my instructions and move toward the treat. If the card lands on D, you'll disobey my instructions and move backward.

Read the list of instructions below. After each one, have children toss their cards to determine if they will obey or disobey the instructions. Encourage them to use the landmarks to remember which lines they started from.

● Hop up two lines.

● Tiptoe up one line.

● Step forward one line, squat down, then stand up.

● Shuffle up two lines.

● Walk like a robot, and move up one line.

● Turn in a circle as you move up two lines.

● Wave to me as you step up one line.

● Give a Tarzan yell as you move up two lines.

● Jump like a frog, and move up two lines.

● Wave your arms like angel wings, and move up one line.

● Pretend you're an ice skater, and glide up one line.

● Bounce up two lines.

● Wiggle your shoulders, and move up one line.

● Pretend you're balancing an elephant on your head, and move up one line.

● Clap your hands, bark like a seal, and move up two lines.

Repeat the list until everyone has reached the treat. Then gather the children in a circle, pass out the treats, and say: **We played this game to help us understand something that happened to a Bible character named Jonah. God asked Jonah to do some-**thing, but Jonah did the opposite of what God asked. Let's tell each other the story of Jonah.

Have children take turns telling the story of Jonah. Ask:

● **Why did Jonah disobey God?**

● **What happens when we disobey?**

Say: **Jonah disobeyed at first, but eventually he did what God asked. When Jonah became a treat for a big fish, he learned that it's best to obey God promptly. It's important for us to obey God, too. God wants us to be quick to obey him.**

Pray: **God help us to keep our cards on the "O" side. Help us to listen and obey you quickly. Thanks for the best treat of all: your love! Amen.**

Have children take their "O and D" cards home. Encourage them to place them on the "O" side every day.

JONAH
2:1–4:11

THEME:
God loves everyone.

SUMMARY:
In this CREATIVE STORYTELLING activity, children see that God cares for everyone.

Assign one child to be Jonah, one child to be the king, one child to be the plant, and three children to be the big fish. All the other children can be the citizens of Nineveh.

Have the king and the citizens of Nineveh stand together on one side of the room. Have the plant kneel on another side of the room. Have the children who are playing the fish hold hands and surround Jonah.

When all the children are in place, say: **For this play, I'll read all the words and you will act out the story. Listen carefully to the words that I emphasize so you'll know what to do.**

Be prepared to prompt children if they're slow in picking up their cues. The cues are underlined in the story.

The story begins with Jonah in the belly of a big fish. Jonah had been inside the fish for three days, then he prayed to God and promised to obey. So God told the fish to spit Jonah out. After the fish spit Jonah onto the dry ground, God spoke to Jonah again, saying, "Get up and go to Nineveh. Tell them what I tell you to say."

So Jonah got up, dusted himself off, and went to the big city of Nineveh. Jonah walked right into the middle of town and preached to the people. Jonah said, "After forty days, Nineveh will be destroyed. God is displeased with your sinful ways."

The people of Nineveh listened and believed. They stopped eating to show how sorry they were for their sins. Even the king was sorry. He got up from his throne, took off his luxurious robe, and put on itchy, rough cloth. Then he sat down in a pile of ashes to show how upset he was.

The king made a decree. He said, "No one is allowed to eat or drink. Everyone, even the animals, must be covered with rough cloth. We will cry loudly to God. Everyone must turn away from evil living and kneel in prayer. Maybe then God will stop being angry with us."

When God saw that the people were sorry for their sins, he changed his mind. God decided not to punish them.

But this made Jonah angry. He wanted God to punish the citizens of Nineveh. Jonah said to God, "I ran away before because I knew what would happen. I knew that if I obeyed you, then the people of Nineveh would repent, and you would decide not to punish them. This makes me so angry that it would be better for me to die."

Then Jonah went out of the city. He built a small shelter for himself and sat in the shade, waiting to see what would happen to Nineveh. God made a plant grow very quickly next to the shelter. It provided more shade and made Jonah more comfortable.

The plant made Jonah very happy. But the next day, the plant shriveled up and died.

Then God sent a hot wind, and Jonah became hot and weary. Jonah was angry that the plant had died. He pouted and said, "It would be better for me to just die."

God said to Jonah, "Do you think it is right for you to be

angry about the plant?"

Jonah said, "Yes, it is right for me to be angry. The plant made me comfortable. Now it's gone and I'm too hot. I'm so angry I could die."

Then God said, "You are so concerned for a plant that was here one day and gone the next. You didn't even help grow the plant. If your concern for the plant is so great, isn't it right that I should care for the thousands of people in Nineveh?"

JONAH
3:1-3

THEME:
God desires our obedience.

SUMMARY:
With this rhythmic CREATIVE STORYTELLING idea, kids understand the importance of obeying God.

Say: **This story is like the singsong pantomime game Going on a Bear Hunt. You'll repeat everything I say and do.** Have kids repeat line by line your words and actions.

(Sit in a chair and imitate walking by slapping thighs with open palms.) **I'm going on a Jonah walk.**

(Push palms outward.) **God said, "Stop, Jonah!"**

(Shake finger.) **"Preach in Nineveh today."**

(Shake head.) **Jonah said, "No way!"**

(Slap thighs as if running.) **Jonah disobeyed 'cause Jonah ran away.**

(Continue to slap thighs.) **Going on a Jonah walk.**

(Pretend to row.) **Jonah boards a boat.**

(Row and rock from side to side.) **A storm rocks the boat.**

Jonah said, "I've sinned," and **the crew threw Jonah in.** *(Jump up and pretend to toss a man overboard.)*

(Make swimming motions.) **Jonah tries to swim.**

(Make loud gulp and hold cheeks with palms of hands.) **But he's swallowed by a fish!**

(Hold up three fingers.) **Jonah sat three days in the belly of that fish.**

(Bow head and clasp hands in prayer.) **Jonah says, "Forgive me, Lord."**

(Hold thumb up.) **God says, "OK, I'll set you free today!"**

The whale spits Jonah out. *(Hold nose.)* **Pew-wee, Jonah, you smell like a fish!**

(Slap thighs as if walking.) **Going on a Jonah walk.**

(Face palms outward.) **God said, "Stop, Jonah!"**

(Shake finger.) **"Preach in Nineveh today."**

(Nod head.) **Jonah said, "OK!"**

(Slap thighs as if running.) **Jonah ran to town.**

(Continue to slap thighs.) **He didn't mess around.**

(Shake finger.) **Jonah told the people,**

(Continue to shake finger.) **"Hear what I say."**

(Point upward.) **"When God says what to do . . .**

(Cup hand around ear and nod.)
"Listen and obey!"

Ask:

● **What did Jonah do when God asked him to go to Nine- veh?**

● What happened when Jonah did not obey God?

● Why is it important to obey God?

● When should we disobey God?

● What are some things you can do to obey God today?

Micah

"The Lord has told you, human, what is good;
he has told you what he wants from you: to do
what is right to other people, love being kind to
others, and live humbly, obeying your God."

Micah 6:8

MICAH
5:2-5a

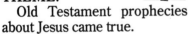

THEME:
Old Testament prophecies about Jesus came true.

SUMMARY:
Have a PARTY to celebrate the prophecies that came true when Jesus was born.

PREPARATION: You'll need boxes of Christmas decorations, a Bible, a wall map of Bible lands, a small photograph of a baby, masking tape, cupcakes, decorative candies, fruit punch, paper cups, and napkins.

Any time is a great time to celebrate God's faithfulness in fulfilling the prophecies about Jesus' birth. For an icebreaker, set out boxes of Christmas decorations, and let kids decorate the room.

Read aloud Micah 5:2-5a. Put a map of Bible lands on the wall. Put a masking tape loop on the back of a picture of a baby. Blindfold the children and play Pin the Baby on Bethlehem. Play until all the children have had a chance. When the game is over, tape the picture on Bethlehem and say: **It was fun to try to put the baby in the right place. God told his people more than seven hundred years before Jesus' birth exactly where Jesus would be born. The little town of Bethlehem was the chosen place.**

To commemorate the gathering of families described in Micah and in Luke 2, play Gathering the Family. Have everyone scatter. Say: **If there's an "a" in your name, hop to the window. If there's an "h" in your name, crawl to the door.** Continue until you've mentioned every letter in the alphabet. Call out directions rapidly so the children are going in several directions at once.

Set out cupcakes, and let kids decorate them. When the cupcakes are decorated, gather everyone together and teach this song to the tune of "Happy Birthday to You."

> Dear God, we love you.
> Your prophecy came true
> When Jesus was born
> On the first Christmas morn'.

Let children enjoy their cupcakes and punch, then end the party with a prayer of thanks to God for his faithfulness.

MICAH
6:6-8

THEME:
Serving others pleases God.

SUMMARY:
In this SERVICE PROJECT, children see that pleasing God can be as simple as providing for others' needs.

PREPARATION: You'll need a Bible and supplies for the activities you choose to do.

Contact a local shelter or food pantry, and find out what kinds of donations they need most. Many places need school supplies; toiletries; and warm clothing, such as coats, hats, and mittens.

Read aloud Micah 6:6-8. Ask:
● **What do you think God most wants from us?**
● **What does it mean to love being kind to others?**
● **How can we live humbly?**
Say: **For the next several weeks, we're going to collect items that many people in our city need, but don't have. It will be our way of being fair and doing right to others.**

Have children launch this program church-wide by writing a note to the congregation. Have the note inserted in the following week's bulletins. Also have children help make an announcement during the worship service. Older children will enjoy going on a scavenger hunt in the neighborhood around the church to collect donations. Have an adult sponsor accompany each group as they collect items. Encourage families to save their spare change to purchase additional items.

Have children help make a display area for the items you collect. If you collect soap bars, you may want to set up the bars on end in the fellowship hall as though they were dominoes. If you collect hats and mittens, string a clothesline around the perimeter of your sanctuary or near the ceiling in the foyer. Clothespin each set of hat and mittens to the clothesline. If you collect school supplies, you could hang a construction paper desk on the wall representing each set collected.

Run the program for four consecutive weeks. If possible, have children help load the supplies and take them to the chosen center.

To complete the project, have children make a report to the congregation stating how much they collected and what they learned from the experience. Let children write and design a thank you note to insert into the bulletins after their mission is accomplished.

NAHUM

"The Lord is good, giving protection in times of trouble. He knows who trusts in him."

Nahum 1:7

NAHUM 1:2-8

THEME:
God is just.

SUMMARY:
On this field TRIP, children see that a just and loving God must enforce rules and punish those who disobey.

PREPARATION: You'll need a Bible.

Arrange to have a traffic officer meet with the children in the church parking lot to talk about bicycle and pedestrian safety. Have the officer explain why it's as important for children to obey the

law as it is for adults.

Then take the children to a place where they can safely watch a busy intersection. Ask children to observe the drivers—to watch and see if drivers use their turn signals, stop at the red lights, and turn from the correct lanes. Also encourage children to see if the drivers are courteous, if bicycle riders signal appropriately, and if pedestrians cross only in the crosswalks. After returning to the classroom, ask:

● **Why do we have traffic laws?**

● **If a person breaks the law, should a police officer give him or her a ticket? Why or why not?**

● **What might happen if the police started ignoring people who broke the law?**

Say: **Sometimes people think that if God really loved us, he** wouldn't punish us when we sin. **Listen to this passage from the Bible.**

Have children take turns reading Nahum 1:2-8 aloud. Ask:

● **What do you think about this passage?**

● **Why do you think God makes rules for us to follow?**

● **What might happen if God ignored people who broke the rules?**

● **Why does God enforce the rules he makes for us to follow?**

Say: **We know that God loves us. We know that God promises to protect those who love him and who trust him. The Bible tells us that God is good. But God makes rules to keep us safe and to help us follow him. God wants us to follow the rules. People who don't follow traffic rules could get hurt. In the same way, we'll hurt ourselves if we don't follow God's rules. Let's thank God for his rules.**

Pray: **God, thank you for caring about us. Thank you for protecting us when we trust in you. We know that you've created rules to keep us safe and to help us follow you. Help us remember to follow your rules every day. Amen.**

NAHUM
1:15

THEME:
We need to share the good news.

SUMMARY:
In this MISSION project, children publish a newsletter of good news and distribute it.

PREPARATION: You'll need plain paper, a marker, a ruler, scissors, a Bible, pencils, and rubber cement. A book of Christian clip art will add fun and interest.

Divide sheets of plain paper into several different-sized rectangles using a marker and a ruler. You'll need a rectangle for each child, plus one extra. Have children help cut out the rectangles. On one rectangle write the words, "Good News Gazette."

Give each child a rectangle and a pencil.

Say: **Listen to this verse.** Read aloud Nahum 1:15. Say: **Today we're going to be the ones bringing good news and announcing peace.** Ask:

● **What good news can we share with others?**

Allow children to respond. Then encourage them to write messages of good news about God on their rectangles. Encourage them to mention such things as Jesus' birth, Jesus' death and resurrection, or the new life we have in Christ. Invite children to draw small illustrations to complement their words of good news.

When children are finished, lay out clean sheets of paper. Put the rectangle that reads "Good News Gazette" on one sheet, then let children assemble their rectangles on the paper to look like a newspaper. It's OK if the writing goes different directions. Dab a bit of rubber cement on the corners of the rectangles and adhere them to the paper.

Photocopy the newsletters, and have children hand them out in front of your church. After they've distributed the newsletters, ask:

● **How did people react to your messages of good news?**

● **Why is it good to spread good news?**

● **How do you feel when you share good news with others?**

● **What else can you do to announce the news about God's love?**

Encourage children to continue to spread good news during the week.

HABAKKUK

"The Lord is my strength. He makes me like a deer that does not stumble."

Habakkuk 3:19a

HABAKKUK 2:18-20

THEME:
God wants us to worship him only.

SUMMARY:
In this OBJECT LESSON, children see that idols are worthless creations of man.

PREPARATION: You'll need cardboard boxes in various sizes, construction paper, scissors, markers, and tape. You'll also need a Bible.

Set out the supplies. Have children work in groups of three to turn a cardboard box into some kind of technical appliance, such as a radio, a television, a computer, or a CD player. Give them several minutes, and encourage them to make their creations as realistic as possible.

After ten minutes, have groups present their creations to the rest of the class. Then say: **What great work you've all done! Let's see how well your creations operate. Why don't you turn them on?**

The children will giggle or look at you as if you're crazy. Play along. Ask:

● **What do you mean they don't work?**

Say: **The Bible talks about a situation similar to this. Let's find out what happened.**

Have a volunteer read aloud Habakkuk 2:18-20. Ask:

● **Why do you think people**

built idols?

● Why is it wrong to build and worship idols?

Say: In other parts of the world, many people build and worship idols even today. In our culture, not many people worship statues, but we have other kinds of idols—things that we put ahead of God. Ask:

● What kinds of things become our idols?

● Why is it just as silly to have our version of idols as it is to worship a man-made statue?

● The last verse of this passage says that all the earth should be silent in the presence of God. What do you think that means?

Say: An idol is anything that we worship other than God. We worship something when we give it more importance than we give God. We know that it's silly to expect a cardboard computer to work. It's just as silly to expect a wooden statue to answer prayers and wishes. God is the only true God. He's the only one worthy of our worship.

Encourage kids to leave their creations on display in the classroom as a reminder of how silly it is to put other things before God.

HABAKKUK 3:3b-6

THEME:
God is great and powerful.

SUMMARY:
With this MUSIC IDEA, children write a song that expresses the greatness and power of God.

PREPARATION: You'll need a Bible, pencils, and paper.

Say: We know that God is great and powerful. The Bible tells us that. But God's greatness and power mean something a little different to each person. Listen to these verses and see if you see the picture of God the writer makes with his words.

Read aloud Habakkuk 3:3b-6. Ask:

● What does God look like in this passage?

Say: Today you get to write a word picture of what God's greatness and power look like to you. You might see God's greatness as being as deep as the ocean or as vast as outer space. Think for a moment about what God's greatness and power mean to you.

Give children a moment to think. Then form groups of three. Give each group a pencil and a sheet of paper.

Say: To make this activity more fun, let's put your word pictures to music. Think of a simple melody that you know like "Twinkle, Twinkle, Little

Star" or "Jesus Loves Me." Write down your own word pictures. Then as you write down each other's word pictures about God, see if you can write them to fit the notes and melody of a song.

Give children at least ten minutes to write. Then give each group an opportunity to sing its song. Ask kids to explain why they chose the words they did to describe God.

Close with a prayer similar to this one: **God, you used many people to write the Bible, and there are lots of word pictures of you. Help us to see the pictures as we read through the Bible so we can get to know you better every day. Amen.**

ZEPHANIAH

"The Lord your God is with you. The mighty One will save you."

Zephaniah 3:17a

ZEPHANIAH 2:1-3

THEME:
God asks people to change.

SUMMARY:
In this QUIET REFLECTION, children consider how they need to change in order to please God.

PREPARATION: You'll need a Bible and a leaf for each child. Real leaves and construction paper leaves work equally well.

Read aloud Zephaniah 2:1-3. Ask:
• **How does this passage make you feel?**
• **What does God ask us to**
do so that he can grant us forgiveness?

Give each child a leaf. Say: **When we change our behavior or our thinking, we often say that we are "turning over a new leaf." Take a moment to look at your leaf. Use your finger and pretend to write on it the things you'd like to change about yourself—things such as bad habits, wrong thoughts, and other sins.** Give children a moment to consider the things they'd like to change.

Then say: **Now turn your leaves over. The second part of this passage says to do what is right. Now let's consider the good actions and thoughts that we will replace our old sinful ways with. Write them on your leaf with your finger.** Give children a moment to consider the positive actions and thoughts they'd like to adopt.

Then pray: **God, we know that you are a perfect, holy, and just God. It makes you sad when we sin. Thank you for second chances, Lord, and please forgive us for the sins we've confessed today. Help us to truly turn over a new leaf. Amen.**

Have the children take the leaves home as reminders of their commitment to change.

ZEPHANIAH 3:14-20

THEME:
God delivers people.

SUMMARY:
With this MUSIC IDEA, children celebrate God's deliverance of his people.

PREPARATION: You'll need a Bible.

Read aloud Zephaniah 3:14-20. Then have kids join in singing this song to the tune of "Do, Lord."

> **Sing God's people, shout for joy.**
> **The Lord God is with you.**
> **Don't be afraid, and don't give up.**
> **The Lord is sure to save.**
> **He'll shout over you with words of joy.**
> **You'll rest within his love**
> **When that day is here.**

For fun, shout these words:

● After the second line, shout, "Yea!"

● After the fourth line, shout, "Hooray!"

● After the sixth line, shout, "Forever!"

When children know the words, have them sit cross-legged in a circle so that their knees touch their neighbor's knees. While they sing the song, have them gently slap their knees to the beat of the song in this rhythm: On the first two beats, they slap their own knees twice. On the second two beats, they cross hands with both of their neighbors and slap their neighbor's knees twice. Continue this rhythm throughout the song.

HAGGAI

"This is what the Lord All-Powerful says:
Think about what you have done.'"

Haggai 1:5

HAGGAI
1:1-4

THEME:
God desires our complete attention.

SUMMARY:
In this DEVOTION, children discover the importance of putting God first even in the midst of compelling distractions.

PREPARATION: You'll need newspaper, tape, a Bible, and a compelling distraction such as a special food treat or a videotape.

EXPERIENCE
Say: **During the time of Ezra, in the Old Testament, the Jews** had been living in exile in another country. After many years, some of the people returned to Jerusalem and started to rebuild the Temple. Today we're going to do the same thing. We'll "rebuild a temple" right here in our classroom. Let me show you how.

Show children how to tightly roll a sheet of newspaper and tape it so it won't unroll. Then show them how to build a log cabin-style temple. Place two rolls parallel to each other on the floor. Then make a square by placing two rolls on top of the first rolls. Tape them all together.

Assign some children to be Rollers. They'll make the newspaper rolls. Assign some children to be Stackers to stack and hold the rolls securely. Assign other children to be Tapers to tape the rolls

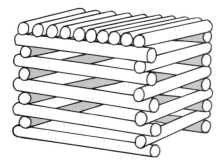

in place. Encourage the Rollers, Stackers, and Tapers to work together to build the temple.

Once children understand how to build the walls of the temple, excuse yourself, saying that you need to prepare the next part of the lesson.

Make a big production of bringing out a special food treat. An even more tempting distraction may be cuing up a video on a television. Be sure it's a show that the children would really enjoy.

Soon some of the children will wander over to the snack or the video monitor. Encourage them to help you with what you're doing. Have them set out napkins or pour juice. Let them help you adjust the volume and tracking of the video. Don't mention finishing the temple.

If no one is distracted, call someone over to help you. One by one call the children away from the temple to help you with your preparations.

RESPONSE

When several or all of the children have left the temple, stop the activity. Gather the children and ask:

● **Why did you decide to leave the temple and come to help me?**
Say: **This is exactly what hap-** pened to the people who were rebuilding the Temple in the Old Testament. They worked hard on the Temple for a while but became distracted by other things that needed to be done. They needed to build homes to live in and they needed to find food to eat and make clothes to wear. Let's find out what the Bible has to say about what they did.

Have children take turns reading aloud Haggai 1:1-4, 7-9. Ask:

● **Why was God dishonored by what the people did?**

● **Is it wrong to build yourself a place to live? Why or why not?**

● **Then why was God disappointed with their actions?**

Say: **We all have many things to do in life. We need to go to school or work, we have chores at home, and we have friends to play with. It's tough to always think of God. Like the people in the Bible story, we often get distracted. But God wants us to focus on him.** Ask:

● **How can we honor God in our lives?**

CLOSING

Say: **To show our intention to honor God in our lives, let's finish the temple we started.**

Have children finish the temple. When the walls are finished and it's time to do the roof, have children make ten to fifteen rolls. Then gather the children together and ask them one by one to lay a roll over the top of the temple walls to create a flat roof. As children each lay rolls on the roof have them mention one way that they can honor God in their lives.

ZECHARIAH

"This is what the Lord All-Powerful says:
'Return to me, and I will return to you.' "

Zechariah 1:3b

ZECHARIAH 4:6

THEME:
God's Spirit helps us.

SUMMARY:
This creative PRAYER helps children appreciate what it means to be helped by God's Spirit.

PREPARATION: You'll need a Bible.

Read aloud Zechariah 4:6. Say: **This activity will help us think about what it's like to be helped by God's Spirit.**

Have children take turns standing in a doorjamb or a corner of the room. For ten seconds, have each child hold their arms rigid and press with their wrists against the doorjamb. Then have them step away from the doorjamb and relax their arms at their sides. Their arms will rise up in the air. This creates the unusual sensation that their arms are lifting miraculously. When everyone has experienced this, ask:

● **How did it feel when you relaxed your arms and they rose in the air?**

● **How is this like when we let God's Spirit work in our lives?**

Have kids stand in a circle with their hands up, palms pressing against their neighbors' palms.

Pray: **Lord God, sometimes our problems seem so great.** Have kids push their hands against each other. **We work so hard to get things done and to make people happy and to solve our** problems. But God, sometimes it seems the harder we work, the less we accomplish.

God, we know when we turn our problems over to you, your Spirit can work amazing things in our lives. Have kids raise their arms to their sides in imitation of the experience they had before. When we let your Spirit work in our lives, we let go of our problems. Thank you for the power your Spirit brings to our lives. Thank you for caring enough to send your Spirit to help us. Amen.

ZECHARIAH
7:8-12

THEME:
God works through soft hearts.

SUMMARY:
This OBJECT LESSON teaches children that we are better servants when our hearts are softened by God's love.

PREPARATION: You'll need Bibles and a new, dry sponge for each child. You'll also need a bucket of soapy water and something dirty to clean such as classroom tables or windows.

This is a good activity to use right after a messy art project.

Give children each a new sponge and say: Let's clean these tables today. They're starting to look dirty. Have children try to clean with the hard, dry sponges. If they ask for cleanser or water, ask them to use the dry sponges for at least thirty seconds. Then have children sit down in a circle and ask:

● Why don't these sponges clean well?

Say: There was a time in the Bible when there was a problem with something else that was as hard as a rock. Listen to Zechariah 7:8-12.

Provide Bibles, and have volunteers take turns reading aloud Zechariah 7:8-12. Then ask:

● What does it mean to have a hard heart?

● How can a heart be softened?

Bring out a bucket of soapy water. Have children immerse their sponges in the water and watch as the sponges expand and soften. Ask:

● Why does a softened sponge work better than a hard sponge?

● Why is a softened heart better than a hard heart?

Dip a sponge in water and say: When our hearts are softened, we see the needs that others have. And when we're full of God's love, we can pour out that love to those who need it. Wring out the sponge over the bucket. You can use your soapy sponges now on these tables that need a good cleaning.

Have children wash the tables. As they work, have them talk about people they know who are hurting. Ask them for ideas about what your class can do to help. Allow children to take the sponges home as reminders to keep their hearts softened to the needs of others.

MALACHI

" 'From the east to the west I will be honored among the nations. Everywhere they will bring incense and clean offerings to me, because I will be honored among the nations,' says the Lord All-Powerful."

Malachi 1:11

MALACHI 1:6-14

THEME:
God wants our best.

SUMMARY:
On this field TRIP, children see what's involved in giving God the best they have.

PREPARATION: Arrange to take children to a local health club or YMCA. If possible, arrange for a fitness instructor to give kids an introduction to the equipment and to lead children in a short aerobic workout.

Take children to a health club to watch people lifting weights or taking an aerobics class. If possible, let children experience a brief workout.

Afterward have kids enjoy a healthy snack, such as orange juice. Ask:

● **What did you notice about the people who were exercising?**

● **How often do you think people come here to exercise?**

● **Why do they work so hard to stay fit and healthy?**

● **What happens when people don't work hard at staying fit and healthy?**

Say: **It's important to work hard at keeping our bodies fit, strong, and healthy. Athletes must give their best to be the best in their sports. It's the same in our relationship to God. During the days when people offered animal sacrifices** to God, God expected them to bring the best animals to be sacrificed. This showed that the people respected God. But some people didn't offer their best. Listen to Malachi 1:6-14.

Have children take turns reading aloud Malachi 1:6-14. Ask:

● How did it cheat God when the people offered animals that weren't perfect?

● We don't offer sacrifices today, but it's still possible to cheat God. How do people cheat God in modern times?

● How do we give our best to God?

Say: No matter what we do in life, we should give it our best effort. But there's one commitment we make that is more important than any other commitment. When we promise to honor God, we're making a promise to the creator of the universe, a holy and perfect God. If we cheat on our promise to God, we're saying that we don't think God is all that important. Let's take a moment to think about our promises to God.

Give children a minute of silence to consider their relationship with God. Then pray: God, we know that you're a holy and great God. There's nothing higher or better than you. We want to give you our very best. Help us to honor you in a way that's pleasing to you. Amen.

MALACHI 4:1-2a

THEME:
God rewards those who honor him.

SUMMARY:
Use this AFFIRMATION ACTIVITY to show children that God rewards those who honor him.

PREPARATION: You'll need a Bible and a flashlight. Punch holes in the bottom of a disposable aluminum pie pan. Plan to do this activity in a room that can be darkened.

Take children into a darkened room, and have them stand in a circle. Turn on the flashlight to read Malachi 4:1-2a aloud. Ask:

● What do you think it means when it says that "goodness will shine on you like the sun"?

● What does it mean when it says, "with healing in its rays"?

Say: People who honor God have nothing to fear. No matter what happens in this world, God will remember us and care for us. Think of the good feeling that comes on a cold day when the sun warms your back. God says that goodness will shine on us like the sun shines on people. Let's explore what that might mean.

Hold the pie pan about twelve inches above a child's head. Hold the flashlight over the pie pan and shine the light through the holes in the pie pan so that the light shines on the child's head. Say: (Child's name) **you honor God by...** Complete the sentence with a personal affirmation for that child. **May goodness shine on you like the healing warmth of sunshine. Continue to honor God each day with your words and actions.**

Complete the first sentence with an affirmation, such as "being patient with everyone" or "speaking kind words to your friends."

Affirm each child in class in the same manner. Older children will enjoy affirming each other.

If it's a sunny day, take children outside and have them sit with their backs to the sun. Have kids close their eyes and enjoy the warmth of the sun. Pray: **God, we thank you for your promises. Help us remember to honor you so that goodness will shine on us like the sun. Amen.**

If it's a cloudy day, have children pretend to feel the warmth of the sun as you pray.

OLD TESTAMENT SCRIPTURE INDEX

OLD TESTAMENT THEME INDEX

obedience—God desires our obedience (Jonah 3:1-3). (p. 181)

obedience—see also RULES

omnipresence—God is with us all the time (Exodus 25:10-22). (p. 39)

omnipresence—God is with us (2 Chronicles 7:1-3). (p. 102)

omnipresence—God is with us everywhere (Jeremiah 23:23-24). (p. 158)

omniscience—God knows all about us (Genesis 17:1-5). (p. 17)

omniscience—God knows the future (Judges 6:33-40). (p. 62)

omniscience—God knows our hearts (Psalm 33:13-22). (p. 122)

P

power—God's power is great (Joshua 6:1-20). (p. 57)

power—Through God's great power, we can do amazing things (Judges 6:11-16). (p. 62)

power—God is powerful (1 Kings 18:18-39). (p. 89)

power—God's power is awesome (Jeremiah 10:12-13). (p. 155)

power—God is great and powerful (Habakkuk 3:3b-6). (p. 190)

praise—We can rejoice in God's goodness (2 Kings 5:1-15). (p. 93)

praise—God enjoys our praise (1 Chronicles 16:31-34). (p. 98)

praise—God wants us to praise him with joy (Nehemiah 12:27-43). (p. 112)

praise—All the people of the world can praise God (Psalm 67). (p. 124)

praise—God desires our praise (Jeremiah 9:23-24). (p. 153)

praise—Harvest is a time to celebrate God (Jeremiah 10:1-6). (p. 154)

praise—We can praise God with music (Jeremiah 32:17). (p. 160)

praise—see also WORSHIP

prayer—We set aside some things as special for God (Leviticus 8:10-12). (p. 41)

prayer—Prayer and praise please God (2 Samuel 22:1-4). (p. 82)

prayer—Prayer is the best way to start everything (1 Chronicles 14:8-12). (p. 97)

prayer—God answers prayer (Nehemiah 2:2-8). (p. 108)

prayer—Patient prayer lets God work (Lamentations 3:21-26). (p. 162)

pride—Pride can cause a fall (Obadiah 3-4). (p. 176)

priorities—God wants us to seek him with our whole heart (Psalm 105:1-5). (p. 128)

promises—God keeps his promises (Genesis 8:18–9:1, 8-17). (p. 14)

promises—God keeps his promises (Joshua 2:2-21). (p. 56)

prophecy—Old Testament prophecies about Jesus came true (Micah 5:2-5a). (p. 183)

protection/provision—God protects us because he loves us (Exodus 2:1-10). (p. 28)

protection/provision—God takes care of us (Exodus 2:1-10). (p. 29)

protection/provision—God saves us (Exodus 14:13-14, 21-31). (p. 32)

protection/provision—God gives us what we need (Exodus 16:4, 14-18). (p. 35)

protection/provision—God is our helper (1 Samuel 17:17-50). (p. 75)

protection/provision—God takes care of us (1 Kings 17:2-16). (p. 88)

protection/provision—God is with us (1 Kings 19:11-13a). (p. 90)

protection/provision—The Lord is my shepherd (Psalm 23). (p. 121)

protection/provision—God protects us (Psalm 61:1-4). (p. 123)

protection/provision—God protects us because he loves us (Isaiah 8:12-13). (p. 148)

protection/provision—God protects us (Jeremiah 1:17-19). (p. 152)

protection/provision—God's Spirit helps us (Zechariah 4:6). (p. 196)

provision/see PROTECTION/PROVISION

R

reflection—It's important to remember what God has done in our lives (Joshua 4:1-9). (p. 57)

repentance—Repentance means turning around (Joel 2:12-13). (p. 171)

repentance—God asks people to change (Zephaniah 2:1-3). (p. 192)

righteousness—God alone is righteous (Amos 7:7-9). (p. 174)

rules—God gives us rules so we can live strong lives (Leviticus 19:1-4, 11-13). (p. 42)

rules—God is just (Nahum 1:2-8). (p. 186)

rules—see also OBEDIENCE

S

sacrifice—God rewards our sacrifices (2 Samuel 24:20-25). (p. 82)

service—When we show love to others, we're showing love to God (Leviticus 2:11). (p. 40)

service—We all can serve God (Numbers 3:5-8). (p. 44)

service—God helps get us ready to serve (1 Samuel 3:4-10). (p. 73)

service—Serving others pleases God (Micah 6:6-8). (p. 184)

sharing—God wants us to share with others (2 Chronicles 24:1-14). (p. 104)

sharing—God's love is meant to be shared (Jeremiah 1:4-9). (p. 151)

sharing faith—God wants us to share his Word with others (Nehemiah 8:1-9). (p. 111)

sharing faith—We need to share the good news (Nahum 1:15). (p. 187)

sovereignty—God is in charge of his world (Genesis 11:1-9). (p. 15)

speech—Kind, careful speaking honors God (Proverbs 18:21). (p. 135)

strength—Be strong in the Lord (Joshua 1:5-9). (p. 55)

strength—God's power helps us do hard things (Judges 7:1-22). (p. 63)

strength—see also PROTECTION/PROVISION

submission—God works through soft hearts (Zechariah 7:8-12). (p. 197)

T

temptation—Temptation takes us away from God (Judges 16:4-22). (p. 64)

temptation—God wants us to walk away from temptation (Judges 16:4-31). (p. 65)

thanksgiving—We can give thanks to God (Leviticus 23:39-43). (p. 43)

thanksgiving—see also PRAISE

time—There is a time for everything (Ecclesiastes 3:1-8). (p. 139)

tithing—God wants us to give generously (Nehemiah 10:32-39). (p. 111)

trust—We can trust God (Deuteronomy 1:21-33). (p. 50)

trust—We can trust the Lord (2 Kings 5:1-14). (p. 92)

trust—We can trust God (Jeremiah 17:7-8). (p. 157)

U

uniqueness—God made us wonderfully (Psalm 139:1-16). (p. 130)

uniqueness—God made each of us unique (Song of Solomon 2:1-3). (p. 143)

W

wisdom—God wants us to ask for wisdom (1 Kings 3:16-28). (p. 86)

wisdom—Wisdom is a gift from God (2 Chronicles 1:7-13). (p. 100)

wisdom—Wisdom comes from God (Proverbs 2:1-6). (p. 132)

work—It's wise to work hard (Proverbs 6:6-11). (p. 134)

work—God blesses our work for him (Ecclesiastes 11:6). (p. 141)

worship—God enjoys celebration and worship (2 Samuel 6:1-5, 14-15). (p. 80)

worship—God enjoys it when we worship him through music (Psalm 95:1-7a). (p. 126)

worship—Only God deserves our worship and praise (Psalm 97:1-9). (p. 126)

worship—God wants us to worship him only (Habakkuk 2:18-20). (p. 189)

worship—see also PRAISE

OLD TESTAMENT TEACHING-STYLE INDEX

⚡AFFIRMATION ACTIVITIES

Leviticus 19:1-4, 11-13 (p. 42)
Deuteronomy 28:1-14 (p. 53)
1 Samuel 16:7 (p. 74)
1 Chronicles 11:1-3 (p. 96)
Psalm 8 (p. 120)
Psalm 139:1-16 (p. 130)
Proverbs 18:21 (p. 135)
Song of Solomon 2:1-3 (p. 143)

Jeremiah 1:4-9 (p. 151)
Jeremiah 29:11-13 (p. 159)
Malachi 4:1-2a (p. 199)

✂CRAFTS AND MAKABLES

Genesis 1:1–2:3 (p. 7)
Genesis 12:1-5 (p. 16)
Genesis 24:10-27 (p. 20)
Exodus 3:1-10 (p. 30)

Exodus 14:13-14, 21-31 (p. 32)
Exodus 16:4, 14-18 (p. 35)
Leviticus 8:10-12 (p. 41)
Numbers 3:5-8 (p. 44)
Deuteronomy 6:4-9 (p. 51)
Joshua 2:2-21 (p. 56)
Joshua 4:1-9 (p. 57)
1 Samuel 18:1-4 (p. 78)
1 Kings 11:7-13 (p. 87)
Job 1:13-22 (p. 117)
Psalm 97:1-9 (p. 126)
Proverbs 2:1-6 (p. 132)
Isaiah 1:18 (p. 147)
Isaiah 55:10-11 (p. 149)
Jeremiah 18:3-6 (p. 158)
Jeremiah 31:3 (p. 160)
Hosea 11:1-4 (p. 169)

CREATIVE STORYTELLING
Genesis 2:8–3:24 (p. 8)
Genesis 27:1-33 (p. 22)
Exodus 2:1-10 (p. 28)
Numbers 14:1-20 (p. 46)
Judges 7:1-22 (p. 63)
1 Kings 18:18-39 (p. 89)
Daniel 3:1-30 (p. 166)
Daniel 6:1-28 (p. 167)
Jonah 2:1–4:11 (p. 179)
Jonah 3:1-3 (p. 181)

DEVOTIONS
Genesis 8:18–9:1, 8-17 (p. 14)
Genesis 18:1-16; 21:1-3 (p. 18)
Exodus 3:11-12; 4:1-17 (p. 31)
Exodus 25:10-22 (p. 39)
Joshua 6:1-20 (p. 57)
Judges 16:4-22 (p. 64)
1 Samuel 1:24-28 (p. 72)
2 Samuel 24:20-25 (p. 82)
2 Kings 21:19-24; 22:1, 8 (p. 94)
Ezra 10:1-3 (p. 106)
Nehemiah 10:32-39 (p. 111)
Psalm 23 (p. 121)
Psalm 61:1-4 (p. 123)
Proverbs 13:20 (p. 135)
Ecclesiastes 7:5 (p. 140)
Jeremiah 1:17-19 (p. 152)
Amos 5:24 (p. 173)
Obadiah 3-4 (p. 176)
Haggai 1:1-4 (p. 194)

LEARNING GAMES
Genesis 11:1-9 (p. 15)
Genesis 17:1-5 (p. 17)

Exodus 1:8-22 (p. 27)
Numbers 5:5-7 (p. 45)
Numbers 9:15-23 (p. 45)
Deuteronomy 8:1-10 (p. 52)
Joshua 24:14-15 (p. 59)
Judges 6:33-40 (p. 62)
Ruth 1:3-18 (p. 68)
1 Samuel 3:4-10 (p. 73)
2 Chronicles 1:7-13 (p. 100)
Nehemiah 4:1-23 (p. 110)
Psalm 33:13-22 (p. 122)
Psalm 105:1-5 (p. 128)
Psalm 127 (p. 130)
Proverbs 27:2 (p. 138)
Ecclesiastes 3:1-8 (p. 139)
Jeremiah 23:23-24 (p. 158)
Joel 2:12-13 (p. 171)
Jonah 1–4 (p. 178)

MUSIC IDEAS
Genesis 21:1-8 (p. 19)
Genesis 45:1-15 (p. 24)
Exodus 20:1-17 (p. 36)
2 Samuel 6:1-5, 14-15 (p. 80)
2 Kings 5:1-15 (p. 93)
1 Chronicles 23:1-6 (p. 99)
Nehemiah 12:27-43 (p. 112)
Psalm 95:1-7a (p. 126)
Psalm 119:9-16 (p. 129)
Proverbs 23:22-25 (p. 137)
Jeremiah 32:17 (p. 160)
Ezekiel 1:22-28; 3:12 (p. 164)
Habakkuk 3:3b-6 (p. 190)
Zephaniah 3:14-20 (p. 193)

OBJECT LESSONS
Genesis 6:5-22 (p. 11)
Leviticus 23:39-43 (p. 43)
Judges 6:11-16 (p. 62)
Ruth 3:10-15 (p. 69)
2 Kings 5:1-14 (p. 92)
2 Chronicles 9:22-28 (p. 103)
Ecclesiastes 12:13-14 (p. 142)
Isaiah 8:12-13 (p. 148)
Isaiah 53:4-6 (p. 149)
Jeremiah 10:12-13 (p. 155)
Amos 7:7-9 (p. 174)
Habakkuk 2:18-20 (p. 189)
Zechariah 7:8-12 (p. 197)

PARTIES
Joshua 1:5-9 (p. 55)
Ruth 4:14-22 (p. 70)
1 Kings 3:4-15 (p. 85)

◆ PRAYERS AND
✋ QUIET REFLECTIONS

🖐 SERVICE PROJECTS
AND MISSIONS

🎭 SKITS

◈ TRIPS 'N' TRAVELS